MINCEUR
ITALIENNE

Ex Libris

Arma virumque cano, Troiae qui primus ab oris

Italiam fato profugus Laviniaque venit

litora, multum ille et terris iactatus et alto

vi superum saevae memorem Iunonis ob iram,

multa quoque et bello passus, dum conderet urbem

inferretque deos Latio, genus unde Latinum

Albanique patres atque altae moenia Romae.

AENEIDOS, Liber I, I-VII

MINCEUR ITALIENNE

SLIMMING GOURMET MENUS AND RECIPES

by

Beverly Cox

Decorations by

Gordon McKellar Black

The Vanguard Press
New York

We wish to acknowledge the
invaluable assistance of
Toni Fitch

Copyright © 1979 by Beverly Cox.
Published simultaneously in Canada by Gage Publishing Co., Agincourt, Ontario.
Library of Congress Catalogue Card Number: 79-63111
ISBN: 0-8149-0820-9
Designer: Tom Torre Bevans
Manufactured in the United States of America.

Foreword

Minceur Italienne is an outgrowth of my first book, *Gourmet Minceur: A Week of Slimming Cuisine*. As in *Gourmet Minceur*, my goal has been to show that dishes using the new French cooking principles can be successfully and deliciously executed by the interested non-professional cook, with ingredients readily available throughout the United States.

Though trained in French cooking, I have long appreciated the cuisine of Italy, for it was from Italian influence that many French dishes evolved. When the Medicis, first Catherine and later Marie, became Queens of France, they brought with them their finest chefs, especially those expert in sauces and pastry. They also introduced new varieties of fruits and vegetables, hitherto unknown in France.

To the Medicis and their chefs we owe such basics of French cooking as béchamel sauce, millefeuille pastry, and even petits pois! Therefore it seemed only fair that the new principles of lighter, more modern cooking developed by France's finest contemporary chefs should travel south.

Minceur Italienne is made up of luncheons, dinners, and antipasti from the major regional cuisines of Italy. Generally, Italian cuisine is divided into Northern and Southern in three ways: meat consumption, cooking fats, and types of pasta.

In the more prosperous regions of the North, meat plays an important role in the daily diet. More butter is used and the pasta is of the softer, flat-noodle variety such as Fettuchini and Lasagna. In the South, cooks rely more on vegetable and seafood dishes. Olive oil is used instead of butter, and pasta is of the harder, tubular variety such as spaghetti and macaroni.

Within this general framework the cooking of each region has its own identity. Our journey through Italy will take us from the Piedmont, famous for its Fontina cheese, grissini (breadsticks), and prohibitively expensive white truffles, to Sicily, an island of citrus groves where the influence of Saracen invaders is seen in the use of exotic seasonings and luscious desserts.

All recipes, except those for sherbets and antipasti, are designed to serve four. Although cuisine minceur is more concerned with the calorie counter, I have also included approximate carbohydrate counts for those who are interested.

Some of the recipes are my slimming adaptations of traditional regional dishes, while others are recipes that have resulted from experimentation with ingredients and flavors of these regions. In developing recipes, I have used minceur principles as much as possible without sacrificing authentic tastes. Very fresh ingredients are used. Sauces are thickened with vegetable purées instead of flour. Cream is replaced by lighter enrichments of low-fat ricotta, cottage cheese, or yogurt. But small amounts of olive oil, butter and, of course, pasta are allowed.

No artificial sweeteners have been used in these recipes, though you may substitute them if you wish. I have most often chosen to use honey because of its concentrated sweetness and healthful nature.

Successful and stimulating dieting depends very much on proper menu planning. When a balance of higher and lower calorie dishes is maintained, we can stay within 1000 calories per day and still enjoy *la dolce vita*.

—B. C.

About the Recipes

Servings and Sizes

All recipes serve four, except for those noted. Calories and carbohydrates are per portion.

All vegetables, fruits, and eggs will be of medium size, unless otherwise indicated.

HERBS

The only fresh ingredients that may be difficult to find at the market are some of the herbs. Though dried herbs may, in some recipes, be used instead of fresh, I think you will enjoy having a window herb garden of your own. Sweet basil, mint, thyme, rosemary, chives, and other herbs can be found in many nurseries or can be grown from seed.

Herbs can be preserved for use during the winter by freezing. To prepare herbs for freezing, pick over and discard any bruised leaves. Place herbs in a saucepan and cover with cold water. Blanch by bringing water to a boil over a high heat and boil for 8 seconds. Then drain and plunge herbs into cold water. Drain and dry with paper towels. Seal in plastic wrap and freeze.

Basil can also be preserved by brushing leaves with olive oil on both sides and placing in rows between sheets of waxed paper. Wrap paper in plastic wrap and freeze. Individual leaves can be peeled off and used as needed.

The dry mixture called Italian Seasonings is available in the spice departments of most grocery stores. It can be a useful substitute for fresh herbs.

ITALIAN CALORIE COUNTER

The following ingredients are frequently used in this book and, generally, in Italian cooking. Since, in some recipes, you may want to increase amounts to suit your taste, I feel that the calorie and carbohydrate counts for small amounts of these staples may prove useful.

Pasta:
a. Noodles, 1 oz. dry = ½ cup cooked *al dente* = 100 calories, 18.6 gr. carbohydrates

b. Spaghetti, 1 oz. dry = ½ cup cooked *al dente* = 108 calories, 21.9 gr. carbohydrates

Ricotta:
1 Tb whole milk = 25 calories, 0.6 gr. carbohydrates

1 Tb part skim = 23 calories, 0.6 gr. carbohydrates

Parmesan cheese:
1 Tb grated = 31 calories, 0.2 gr. carbohydrates

Romano cheese:
1 Tb grated = 29 calories, 0.2 gr. carbohydrates

Eggs:
1 medium = 71 calories, 0.4 gr. carbohydrates

Olive oil:
1 Tb = 126 calories, 0. gr. carbohydrates

Butter:
1 Tb = 100 calories, 0.1 gr. carbohydrates

Honey:
1 Tb = 61 calories, 16.5 gr. carbohydrates

Onions:
1 Tb chopped = 4 calories, 1.0 gr. carbohydrates

Capers:
1 Tb = 6 calories, 1.0 gr. carbohydrates

Tomato paste:
1 Tb = 12 calories, 2.4 gr. carbohydrates

Anchovies:
a. 1 filet = 3 calories, 0 gr. carbohydrates

b. 1 Tb paste = 20 calories, 1.0 gr. carbohydrates

Italy

Table of Contents

Liguria

LUNCHEON   49

Trenette al Pesto   50
NOODLES WITH PESTO SAUCE

Pesche Ripiene alla Ligure   51
STUFFED PEACHES LIGURIAN STYLE

DINNER   52

Zuppa di Pomodoro   53
CREAM OF TOMATO SOUP

Filetti di Pesce e Spinaci in Cartoccio   54
FISH FILETS AND SPINACH IN PAPER CASES

Spinaci alla Genovese   55
SPINACH GENOVESE STYLE

Gelato di Fragole   56
STRAWBERRY ICE

Emilia-Romagna

LUNCHEON   59

Gnocchi Verdi con Salsa di Ricotta   60
SPINACH DUMPLINGS IN RICOTTA SAUCE

Fragole in Paniere di Arance   61
STRAWBERRIES IN ORANGE BASKETS

DINNER   62

Zuppa alla Modenese   63
SPINACH SOUP MODENESE STYLE

Petti di Pollo al Marsala   64
BREAST OF CHICKEN MARSALA

Mele alla Francese   65
APPLE SOUFFLÉ

Tuscany

LUNCHEON   67

Insalata di Fagiolini e Cipolle   68
GREEN BEAN AND ONION SALAD

Frittata di Tonno   69
TUNA OMELETTE WITH YOGURT SAUCE

Budino di Ricotta   70
RICOTTA PUDDING

DINNER   71

Tagliatelle con Salsa di Broccoli   72
NOODLES WITH BROCCOLI SAUCE

Bistecca alla Fiorentina   73
BEEFSTEAK FLORENTINE

Gelato di Melone   74
MELON ICE

Umbria and the Marches

LUNCHEON   77

Insalata di Finocchio e Rucola   78
FENNEL AND ARUGULA SALAD

Spaghetti Aglio ed Olio   79
SPAGHETTI WITH OIL, GARLIC, AND GINGER

Zabaione Semi Freddo   79
FROZEN WINE CUSTARD

DINNER   80

Pollo alla Perugina   81
ROAST CHICKEN WITH FENNEL

Pomodori al Forno   82
BAKED TOMATO HALVES

Crespelle di Ciliege   83
CHERRY CREPES

Latium

LUNCHEON   85

Pomodori Ripieni Primavera   86
TOMATOES STUFFED WITH RICE
AND SPRING VEGETABLES

Melone Cantalupo   87
CANTALOUPE

DINNER   88

Stracciatella   89
ROMAN CONSOMMÉ

Vitello Tonnato   90
COLD VEAL WITH TUNA FISH SAUCE

Mele al Vino Rosso   91
APPLES POACHED IN RED WINE

Abruzzi and Molise

LUNCHEON   93

Insalata di Crescione   94
WATERCRESS SALAD

Timballo di Pollo e Spinaci   95
CHICKEN AND SPINACH TORT

Formaggio Pecorino e Pere   96
PECORINO CHEESE AND PEAR

DINNER   97

Fettuccine in Salsa   98
FETTUCCINI WITH FRESH VEGETABLES

Bracioline d'Agnello   99
LAMB CHOPS

Granita di Caffe   99
COFFEE ICE

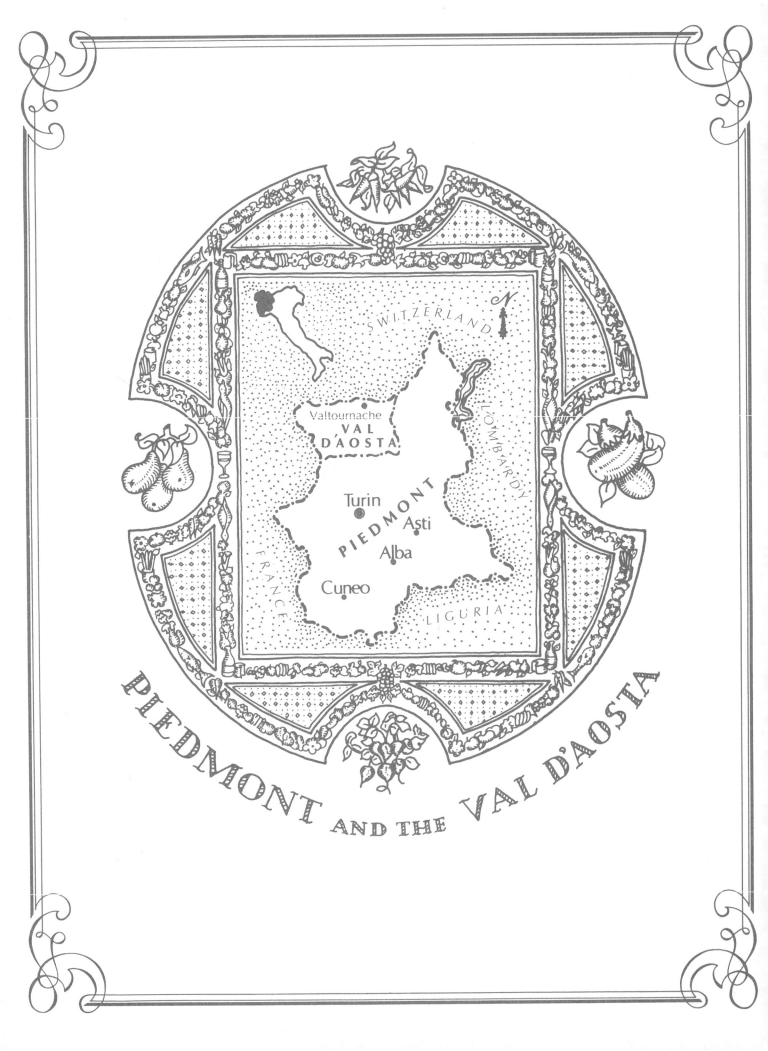

PIEDMONT AND THE VAL D'AOSTA

LUNCHEON

Insalata di Topinambur e Crescione

JERUSALEM ARTICHOKE AND WATERCRESS SALAD · 73 CALORIES · 8.1 GR. CARBOHYDRATES

Lasagna Piemontese

LASAGNA PIEDMONT STYLE · 295 CALORIES · 38.4 GR. CARBOHYDRATES

Fragole Marsalate

STRAWBERRIES WITH MARSALA · 53 CALORIES · 13.0 GR. CARBOHYDRATES

Total
Calories
421

Total
Carbohydrates
59.5 gr.

Insalata di Topinambur e Crescione

JERUSALEM ARTICHOKE AND WATERCRESS SALAD
73 CALORIES · 8.1 GR. CARBOHYDRATES

INGREDIENTS

½ lb. Jerusalem artichokes with as few knobs as possible
A bowl of cold acidulated water (1 Tb lemon juice per 2 cups cold
    water)
½ lb. watercress
Salt and freshly ground pepper
2 Tb olive oil
2 tsp red wine vinegar

METHOD

1. Soak artichokes in cold water. Peel and toss into a bowl of acidulated cold water to prevent discoloration.

2. Wash watercress and remove any tough stems. Blot dry gently with paper towels and place in a salad bowl.

3. When ready to serve, remove artichokes from acidulated water and pat dry.

4. Slice artichokes thinly and add to salad bowl.

6. Sprinkle with salt and pepper to taste and add oil and vinegar.

7. Toss lightly and arrange salad on 4 salad plates.

Lasagna Piemontese

LASAGNA PIEDMONT STYLE · 295 CALORIES · 38.4 GR. CARBOHYDRATES

INGREDIENTS

5 wide Lasagna noodles = ¼ package
2 qt. boiling water
2 tsp salt
2 tsp olive oil

Tomato Sauce:
½ tsp olive oil
½ tsp butter
¾ cup chopped onion
1 cup coarsely chopped mushrooms
1 small pork link sausage, sliced in thin rounds
1 lb. ripe flavorful fresh tomatoes peeled and cored or 1 lb. whole canned Italian-style tomatoes
⅓ cup tomato sauce or juice from Italian-style canned tomatoes

2 tsp chopped fresh basil or ½ tsp dried
1 Tb chopped parsley
Salt and pepper

Spinach Mixture:
1 lb. package fresh spinach or 10 oz. chopped defrosted frozen
2 tsp minced garlic
2 medium egg yolks
⅔ cup low-calorie cottage cheese
Salt and pepper
1 oven-proof baking dish, 4 × 6 inches long and 3 inches deep, lightly oiled
1¼ cup sliced mushrooms
1½ tsp grated Parmesan cheese

METHOD

1. Bring water to a rolling boil. Add salt, olive oil, and noodles. Boil pasta for 10 minutes or until tender but still firm.

2. Carefully transfer noodles to a bowl of cold water to cool, then drain on paper towels.

3. Melt olive oil and butter in a non-stick skillet and stir in onions. Cook over medium heat, stirring often with a wooden spatula until soft and lightly browned.

4. Add chopped mushrooms and sausage to onions. Continue cooking, stirring often, for two minutes more, then add tomatoes, tomato sauce, basil, and parsley and simmer over low heat for five minutes more, using spatula to crush tomatoes. Reserve tomato sauce and prepare spinach mixture.

5. Wash spinach, removing large, tough stems. Cook spinach in a heavy covered saucepan with only the washing water on the leaves until spinach is just wilted, then drain and squeeze out remaining water.

6. Blend spinach, garlic, egg yolks, and cottage cheese in a blender or food processor until it becomes a creamy paste. Add salt and pepper to taste.

7. Preheat oven to 350°. Line the bottom of the baking dish with a layer of noodles.

8. Spoon in ⅔ of tomato sauce and a layer of fresh mushrooms. Sprinkle with ½ tsp grated Parmesan.

9. Follow with another layer of noodles, ⅔ of spinach mixture, and a layer of sliced mushrooms. Sprinkle with ½ tsp Parmesan.

10. Add a final layer of noodles. Cover one side of the top layer with spinach mixture and the other side with tomato sauce.

11. Cover dish with foil and bake for 25 minutes in preheated 350° oven.

Fragole Marsalate

STRAWBERRIES WITH MARSALA · 53 CALORIES · 13.0 GR. CARBOHYDRATES

INGREDIENTS

1 pt. fresh strawberries
⅔ cup fresh orange juice
1 Tb Marsala

Garnish:
Fresh Mint

METHOD

1. Wash and slice strawberries or leave whole, if you wish.

2. Keep 4 whole strawberries with stems as garnish.

3. Combine strawberries, orange juice, and Marsala. Chill for at least ½ hour before serving.

4. Serve berry slices in chilled compotes or wine glasses. Garnish with whole berries and fresh mint.

DINNER

Brodo

PIEDMONT-STYLE BROTH · 45 CALORIES · 0.5 GR. CARBOHYDRATES

Bollito con Salsa Verde

MIXED BOILED MEATS WITH GREEN SAUCE · 210 CALORIES · 8.2 GR. CARBOHYDRATES

Formaggio Fontina

FONTINA CHEESE · 168 CALORIES · 0.9 GR. CARBOHYDRATES

Total
Calories
423

Total
Carbohydrates
9.6 gr

Brodo

PIEDMONT-STYLE BROTH · 45 CALORIES · 0.5 GR. CARBOHYDRATES

INGREDIENTS

Cooking broth from bollito (see page 19)
Salt and pepper
2 Tb coarsely chopped fresh basil or 1 Tb minced parsley and ¼
    tsp dry basil

METHOD

1. When meat has been removed from bollito, put broth through a strainer.

2. Discard vegetables and bouquet garni.

3. You should have approximately 4 cups of broth. If you do not, add more water or canned broth.

4. Return broth to a clean saucepan and add salt and pepper to taste.

5. Reheat broth and serve garnished with chopped basil.

Bollito con Salsa Verde

MIXED BOILED MEATS WITH GREEN SAUCE · 45 CALORIES · 0.5 GR. CARBOHYDRATES

INGREDIENTS

2 carrots peeled and quartered
2 onions halved

Bouquet garni in cheese cloth:
6 sprigs parsley
1 small bay leaf
¼ tsp dry Italian Seasonings
1 clove
1 13¾-oz. can beef broth
1 13¾-oz. can chicken broth
4 to 5 cups cold water
½ lb. lean beef steak, boneless chuck or round
1 whole chicken breast, approximately ½ lb.
1 small pork sausage link

Garnish Preparation:
2 qt. water and 2 tsp salt
¼ lb. green beans washed, ends broken off to remove strings, and cut into 1-inch lengths

3 carrots, peeled and cut into bite-size olive shapes
2 turnips, peeled and cut into bite-size olive shapes
1 Tb minced parsley

Salsa Verde (Sauce Ingredients):
⅓ cup minced parsley
2 tsp capers
2 tsp minced gherkins (French cornichon style)
1 pinch sugar
½ tsp minced garlic
1 tsp Dijon-style mustard
2 Tb broth

METHOD

1. Combine vegetables, bouquet garni, broth, and 3 cups water in a large saucepan with lid or a Dutch oven, bring to a boil. Add beef and simmer partially covered for 45 minutes.

2. Add chicken, sausage, and enough water to cover and return to a boil. Lower heat and continue to simmer for 25 to 30 minutes or until all meats are tender.

3. Preheat oven to 300°.

4. When meats are tender, remove from broth with a slotted spoon. Discard chicken bones and divide meats into 4 portions. Place meat in an oven-proof serving dish, spoon over 2 or 3

Tb of broth, cover, and keep warm in oven.

5. Bring salted water to a boil, add carrot and turnip pieces, and cook for 4 minutes. Add string beans and continue cooking over high heat for 3 minutes more. Drain.

6. Plunge vegetables into cold water to preserve their color, sprinkle lightly with salt and pepper, and add to meats.

7. Combine sauce ingredients in a food processor or blender and blend until smooth.

8. Serve bollito sprinkled with parsley. Sauce is passed separately.

Formaggio Fontina

FONTINA CHEESE · 168 CALORIES · 0.9 GR. CARBOHYDRATES

INGREDIENTS

1½ oz. Fontina cheese per person

Garnish:
Fresh mint

Fontina comes from the Val d'Aosta. It has a rich orange color and mild taste. Though Fontina is usually considered a cooking cheese in the Piedmont, I find it a very pleasant eating cheese.

METHOD

1. Slice Fontina thin and arrange in a fan shape on a bed of mint.

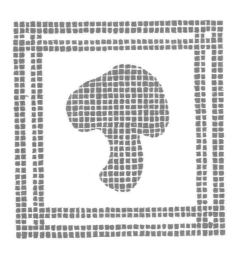

LUNCHEON

Insalata di Endivia

ENDIVE AND BACON SALAD · 51 CALORIES · 3.1 GR. CARBOHYDRATES

Zuppa alla Pavese

CHICKEN CONSOMMÉ WITH POACHED EGG · 153 CALORIES · 9.6 GR. CARBOHYDRATES

Formaggio Bel Paese o Gorgonzola

BEL PAESE OR GORGONZOLA CHEESE · 111 CALORIES · 0.4 GR. CARBOHYDRATES

Total Calories 315

Total Carbohydrates 13.1 gr.

Insalata di Endivia

ENDIVE AND BACON SALAD · 51 CALORIES · 3.1 GR. CARBOHYDRATES

INGREDIENTS

2 whole endives
2 strips bacon
½ tsp minced garlic
2 tsp wine vinegar
2 tsp minced parsley
½ tsp minced fresh mint (optional)

METHOD

1. Wash endives and dry with paper towels.

2. Reserve 12 small whole leaves of endive and cut the rest into bite-size pieces and place in a bowl.

3. Chop bacon into small pieces and fry until brown.

4. Remove bacon with a slotted spoon and sprinkle over cut endive. Reserve 1 Tb of bacon grease.

5. Place garlic, vinegar, and warm bacon grease in a small bowl and whisk together.

6. Pour over endive and bacon and toss lightly.

7. Place 3 whole endive leaves decoratively on each plate. Top with endive and bacon salad and sprinkle with parsley and optional mint.

8. Serve at once.

Zuppa alla Pavese

CHICKEN CONSOMMÉ WITH POACHED EGG · 153 CALORIES · 9.6 GR. CARBOHYDRATES

INGREDIENTS

4 slices diet bread
4 very fresh eggs
1 qt. water
1 Tb white vinegar per quart of water
A large bowl of cold water

3 cups fresh or canned chicken broth
2 Tb grated Parmesan cheese
2 tsp fresh chopped basil or parsley (optional)
Salt, freshly ground pepper
A dash of paprika

METHOD

Note: To poach eggs successfully in the traditional manner, they must be very fresh. If your eggs are not as fresh as you would like, or just for convenience, you may wish to use an egg poacher.

1. Place 2 inches of water, approximately 1 qt., in an 8-to-10 inch flat-bottomed skillet or shallow saucepan. Add 1 Tb vinegar and bring to a simmer.

2. Break 1 egg into a saucer and, holding the saucer very close to the water, slide the egg in.

3. Using a wooden spoon, quickly and gently lift the white over the yolk.

4. Maintaining the water at a simmer, quickly follow the above procedure with the remaining eggs.

5. After 3 minutes, carefully remove the first egg from the water with a slotted spoon and test with your finger. The white should be firm, but the yolk still soft.

6. Place eggs as they are done in a bowl of cold water to stop cooking and wash off any vinegar taste. *Note: Can be done ahead to this point, leaving eggs in cold water several hours in advance.

7. If you have a large biscuit or cookie cutter, cut rounds out of diet bread, otherwise leave slices whole.

8. Toast bread lightly and place one round in the bottom of each soup plate.

9. Carefully remove poached eggs from water and place on a towel to drain. Trim off any ragged edges of white and place eggs on toast rounds.

10. Bring the chicken broth to a slow boil in a saucepan.

11. Sprinkle grated Parmesan, optional basil or parsley, a few grains of salt and pepper, and a dash of paprika over each egg.

12. Carefully pour boiling chicken stock into the soup plates from the side.

13. Serve at once.

Formaggio Bel Paese o Gorgonzola

BEL PAESE OR GORGONZOLA CHEESE · 111 CALORIES · 0.4 GR. CARBOHYDRATES

INGREDIENTS

1 oz. Gorgonzola or 1 oz. of Bel Paese or ½ oz. of each

Garnish:
4 small bouquets of watercress

METHOD

Note: Lombardy is one of the great cheese regions of Italy. Cheese has such importance that special banks exist in several cities of this region where cheese producers deposit actual cheeses in the bank as collateral on loans! The two most important cheeses of Lombardy are Gorgonzola and Bel Paese.

Gorgonzola, with its greenish stripes, looks something like Roquefort, but is made from whole cow's milk rather than sheep's milk, and is more creamy in texture. For those who enjoy a cheese of strength and character, it is a good choice.

Bel Paese, made of whole cow's milk and yellow in color, is a favorite with fanciers of mild cheeses because of its creamy texture and delicate flavor.

1. Serve the cheese or cheeses of your choice at room temperature and garnish plates with small bouquets of watercress.

DINNER

Carciofi alla Milanese

ARTICHOKES MILANESE STYLE · 96 CALORIES · 11.3 GR. CARBOHYDRATES

Osso Buco

BRAISED VEAL SHANKS · 350 CALORIES · 12.6 GR. CARBOHYDRATES

Gelato di Pere

PEAR ICE · 83 CALORIES · 21.0 GR. CARBOHYDRATES

Total Calories 529

Total Carbohydrates 44.9 gr.

Carciofi alla Milanese

ARTICHOKES MILANESE STYLE · 96 CALORIES · 11.3 GR. CARBOHYDRATES

INGREDIENTS

4 artichokes
½ lemon
4 tsp butter
8 tsp grated Parmesan cheese
4 Tb water
Salt and pepper to taste

Garnish:
1 bunch of watercress and 8 small cherry tomatoes
A lightly oiled oven-proof casserole with lid

METHOD

1. Preheat oven to 300°.

2. If possible, break off the stems of artichokes at the base with your hands. This pulls out some of the tough stem fibers that grow into the heart of the artichoke.

3. Lay artichoke on its side. Using a sharp knife, trim off any remaining stem so that artichokes will stand easily.

4. With scissors, trim ½ inch off tips of remaining leaves. Rub all cut sections with lemon.

5. Parboil artichokes for 7 minutes in salted boiling water. Drain and refresh with cold water.

6. Reach into the center of each artichoke and remove the prickly center core of leaves. Using a grapefruit spoon, carefully scrape out the prickly choke.

7. Put 1 tsp of butter into the center of each artichoke and spoon in one tsp of grated Parmesan. Sprinkle one more tsp of Parmesan between the outer leaves.

8. Place artichokes in oiled casserole. Sprinkle lightly with salt and pepper and spoon 1 Tb water over each one. Cover and cook in the middle of preheated 300° oven for 45 to 50 minutes or until you can easily pull off a leaf.

9. Serve artichokes with wreaths of watercress and cherry tomatoes.

Osso Buco

BRAISED VEAL SHANKS · 350 CALORIES · 12.6 GR. CARBOHYDRATES

INGREDIENTS

1 veal shank. Have the butcher saw shank into 4 pieces, approximately 2 inches long (or 1 lb. well-trimmed veal stew meat cut into 2-inch cubes).
1 tsp butter and 1 tsp olive oil
1 cup chopped onion
1 cup chopped carrot
⅔ cup chopped celery
1½ cups canned Italian tomatoes and juice
1 cup beef broth
1 cup dry white wine
½ tsp fresh minced basil
½ tsp dry Italian Seasonings
⅛ tsp pepper

1 large bay leaf
2 Tb minced parsley
Salt to taste

2 cups boiled rice

Gremolada:
2 Tb finely grated lemon rind
2 tsp minced garlic
2 Tb minced parsley

Garnish:
Lemon wedges
Parsley

METHOD

1. Melt butter and oil in a non-stick skillet. Add pieces of veal shank and brown slowly.

2. Remove veal to a large, heavy saucepan with a lid, or a dutch oven.

3. Sauté onion, carrot, and celery in the skillet, then add to veal.

4. Stir in tomatoes and juice, beef broth, white wine, Italian Seasonings, basil, pepper, bay leaf, parsley, and salt to taste.

5. Bring to a boil, then cover and simmer for 1 hour or until veal is tender.

6. While osso buco is simmering, prepare gremolada.

7. When veal is tender, remove it from saucepan and put aside. Discard bay leaf and purée ½ of sauce to achieve a thicker consistency.

8. Return veal and puréed sauce to sauce in saucepan, sprinkle on gremolada, and simmer for 2 or 3 minutes to reheat and blend flavors.

9. Serve osso buco with boiled rice (½ cup per person) and garnish plates with bouquets of parsley and lemon wedges.

Gelato di Pere

PEAR ICE · 83 CALORIES · 21.0 GR. CARBOHYDRATES

INGREDIENTS

4 ripe flavorful pears
8 Tb lemon juice
1½ Tb honey
1⅓ cup water

Garnish:
Fresh mint

METHOD

Note: Pear purée discolors quickly, so make sure that your ice-cream freezer or ice tray is clean and ready to use as soon as sherbet mixture is prepared. Trays should be rinsed with baking soda and water, then scalded with boiling water.

1. Peel a pear, remove core, cut pear into pieces, and toss with lemon juice. Repeat operation with remaining pears.

2. Purée pears, lemon juice, and honey.

3. Stir in cold water and freeze mixture in an ice-cream freezer or an ice tray. If using the ice-tray method, stir mixture several times while it is freezing.

4. Remove sherbet from the freezer and place in the refrigerator at the beginning of your dinner so that it will soften slightly.

5. Serve sherbet in wine or sherbet glasses. Garnish with fresh mint.

AUSTRIA

Bressanone

Merano

Bolzano

Trento

LOMBARDY

VENEZIA EUGENEA

N

VENEZIA TRIDENTINA

LUNCHEON

Cipolle Ripiene

STUFFED ONIONS · 153 CALORIES · 30.3 GR. CARBOHYDRATES

Strudel di Mele

INDIVIDUAL APPLE STRUDELS · 120 CALORIES · 11.0 GR. CARBOHYDRATES

Total Calories 273

Total Carbohydrates 41.3 gr.

Cipolle Ripiene

STUFFED ONIONS · 153 CALORIES · 30.3 GR. CARBOHYDRATES

INGREDIENTS

4 large Bermuda onions—approximately 2.25 lb.
1 tsp butter and 1 tsp oil
⅔ lb. lean ground beef
1 peeled diced tomato
2 Tb minced parsley
4 tsp raisins

Salt, pepper, and nutmeg to taste
2 Tb grated Parmesan cheese
1 oz. Fontina cheese

Garnish:
4 small sprigs of parsley

METHOD

1. Preheat oven to 375°.

2. Using a small, sharp knife, peel and remove the tough outer layer of onion.

3. Then cut a very thin slice off of the bottom of onion so it will stand easily, and a slice approximately ½-inch thick off the top.

4. Using the knife and a small spoon, carefully hollow out the onions until they are only two or three layers thick. If you make a hole in the bottom of an onion don't worry, as it can be patched. Reserve insides of onions.

5. Parboil onion shells in lightly salted water for 2 or 3 minutes or until tender. Carefully remove and drain.

6. Mince 4 Tb of the insides of onions and reserve the rest for other use.

7. Melt 1 tsp butter and 1 tsp oil in a large non-stick skillet. Add minced onion and cook over medium heat until soft but not colored.

8. Add beef to skillet and sauté lightly, breaking up beef with a wooden spoon.

9. Add tomato, parsley, and raisins and cook for a few more seconds, mixing with a wooden spoon.

10. Add salt, pepper, and nutmeg to taste, then sprinkle on grated Parmesan cheese.

11. Try carefully to remove another inner layer or so of onion shells, making them as thin as possible. If there is a hole in the bottom of a shell, patch it with a piece of shell you have removed.

12. Place shells in a lightly oiled baking dish and stuff with meat mixture. Bake in the middle of preheated 375° oven for 15 minutes.

13. Cut Fontina into 8 thin strips.

14. After 15 minutes remove onions from oven and place strips, one across the other, on top of each onion. Return to oven for 5 minutes, or until cheese melts.

15. Place a sprig of parsley on top of each onion and serve.

Strudel di Mele

INDIVIDUAL APPLE STRUDELS · 120 CALORIES · 11.0 GR. CARBOHYDRATES

INGREDIENTS

1½ baking apples
1 Tb lemon juice
1½ Tb butter
1½ tsp honey
¼ tsp grated lemon rind
1½ tsp dark raisins

Pinch of cinnamon
1 small package strudel or filo pastry sheets (available in Greek markets)
1 supple pastry brush
1 teflon-lined muffin tin
½ tsp powdered sugar

METHOD

1. Preheat oven to 375°.

2. Core and peel apples and rub with lemon juice.

3. Melt butter.

4. Cut apples into thin wedges. Toss with 2 tsp melted butter, honey, grated lemon rind, raisins, and cinnamon.

5. Remove 1 sheet of filo pastry from package (dough must be kept tightly sealed and refrigerated or it will dry out).

6. Brush pastry with melted butter and fold in half, buttered sides together.

7. Cut folded sheet in half to form two almost square pieces. Brush one side of each "square" lightly with butter and fit buttered side down into muffin tin with edges overhanging.

8. Fill each of the two pastry-lined cups with ¼ of apple filling, then fold the pastry edges in an overlapping fashion to enclose apple. If necessary, brush on a bit more butter to make edges stick together.

9. Repeat steps 5 through 8 with a second sheet of filo pastry. Then bake strudels in the middle of preheated 375° oven for 15 minutes or until crisp and golden brown.

10. Carefully remove strudels from muffin tins. Sprinkle lightly with powdered sugar and serve slightly warm or at room temperature.

DINNER

Insalata di Ravanelli

RADISH SALAD · 65 CALORIES · 6.6 GR. CARBOHYDRATES

Golasch

TIROLESE BEEF WITH VEGETABLES · 336 CALORIES · 19.6 GR. CARBOHYDRATES

Groviera e Pere

ITALIAN GRUYÈRE CHEESE AND PEAR · 155 CALORIES · 25.2 GR. CARBOHYDRATES

Total
Calories
556

Total
Carbohydrates
51.4 gr.

Insalata di Ravanelli

RADISH SALAD · 65 CALORIES · 6.6 GR. CARBOHYDRATES

INGREDIENTS

10 oz. radishes
1½ tsp olive oil
1¼ tsp wine vinegar
Salt and pepper

Garnish:
8 sprigs watercress or parsley

METHOD

Note: Instructions for carving radish roses can be found in recipe for a "bouquet" of raw vegetables, page 134.

1. Carve 4 radish roses and place in cold water to open.

2. Wash remaining radishes thoroughly, dry, and slice into thin rounds.

3. Sprinkle olive oil and vinegar over radish rounds and toss gently.

4. Season with salt and pepper to taste.

5. Arrange radish slices attractively on four chilled salad plates. Garnish with radish roses and sprigs of watercress.

Golasch

TIROLESE BEEF WITH VEGETABLES · 336 CALORIES · 19.6 GR. CARBOHYDRATES

INGREDIENTS

1 tsp butter and 1 tsp oil
1 cup finely diced onions
1 cup finely diced carrots
1½ tsp paprika
1 lb. very lean boneless beef stew meat, cut into
    1-inch cubes
3 cups beef broth
3 or 4 cups water
Salt and pepper to taste

Garnish:
2 qt. boiling water
1½ cups green beans, washed and cut into
    2-inch lengths
3 or 4 baby carrots per person (washed and
    peeled)
1½ tsp vinegar
1 Tb olive oil
Pinch of sugar
Salt and pepper
2 Tb minced parsley

METHOD

1. Heat butter and oil in a large non-stick skillet, add onion, carrot, and paprika, and cook over medium heat, stirring occasionally until onion is soft and starting to color.

2. Add beef to skillet and brown on all sides, pushing vegetables to one side. Sprinkle lightly with salt and pepper.

3. Add broth and enough water to cover beef. Bring to boil, then lower heat to a simmer. Simmer partially covered for 1 hour or until beef is tender and sauce is fairly thick.

4. 10 minutes before serving, plunge carrots into boiling water, cook for 5 minutes, then add beans and cook for 3 minutes more.

5. Plunge vegetables into cold water to keep fresh color, drain, and toss with vinegar, oil, sugar, salt, and pepper.

6. Divide golasch into 4 portions, arrange vegetables attractively on each plate, and sprinkle with minced parsley.

Groviera e Pere

ITALIAN GRUYÈRE CHEESE AND PEAR · 155 CALORIES · 25.2 GR. CARBOHYDRATES

INGREDIENTS

½ oz. Italian Gruyère cheese per person
1 fresh pear per person

Garnish:
Fresh mint

Similar in taste and texture to Swiss and French varieties, Italian Gruyère is appreciated in the Northern regions.

METHOD

1. Cover dessert plates with paper doilies or a bed of fresh mint. Place a whole pear surrounded with thin slices of cheese on each plate.

AUSTRIA

VENEZIA
TRIDENTINA

LOMBARDY

Vicenza

Verona

Padua

Venice

EMILIA-ROMAGNA

N

PAX TIBI MARCEAE EVAN GELI STA MEUS

PAX TIBI MARCEAE EVAN GELI STA MEUS

VENEZIA EUGENEA

Risi co l' Ueta

RICE WITH RAISINS · 157 CALORIES · 27.3 GR. CARBOHYDRATES

Fegato alla Veneziana

CALF'S LIVER VENETIAN STYLE · 195 CALORIES · 9.0 GR. CARBOHYDRATES

Formaggio Asiago e Mele

ASIAGO CHEESE AND APPLE · 96 CALORIES · 10.3 GR. CARBOHYDRATES

Total
Calories
448

Total
Carbohydrates
46.6 gr.

Risi co l' Ueta

RICE WITH RAISINS · 157 CALORIES · 27.3 GR. CARBOHYDRATES

INGREDIENTS

1½ oz. raisins and ½ cup hot water
1½ cups chicken broth and ¾ cup water
1 tsp olive oil and 1 tsp butter
½ tsp minced garlic
1½ tsp minced parsley
½ cup converted rice
2 Tb grated Parmesan cheese
Salt and pepper

Garnish:
1½ tsp minced parsley

METHOD

1. Soak raisins in hot water to soften.

2. Bring chicken broth and water to a boil.

3. Place oil, butter, garlic, and parsley in a non-stick skillet and sauté lightly.

4. Add rice to skillet and stir until rice is thoroughly coated with oil and lightly sautéed.

5. Add ½ cup boiling stock to rice and transfer to a heavy saucepan, stirring often until broth is absorbed.

6. Continue adding boiling broth ½ cup at a time until rice is tender, but still slightly chewy.

7. Stir in grated cheese. Salt and pepper to taste.

8. Serve with liver Venetian style. Garnish with chopped parsley.

Fegato alla Veneziana

CALF'S LIVER VENETIAN STYLE · 195 CALORIES · 9.0 GR. CARBOHYDRATES

INGREDIENTS

2 medium onions
2 tsp olive oil
1 lb. calf's liver (Have your butcher slice liver very thin—about ⅛ of an inch thick), cut into small pieces approximately the size of a silver dollar

4 or 5 fresh sage leaves or ¼ tsp dry sage
3 Tb minced parsley
Salt and pepper

METHOD

1. Peel and slice onions very thin. Divide into rings.

2. Using a non-stick skillet, sauté onions in olive oil until lightly browned.

3. Add liver and sauté briefly until lightly browned on both sides.

4. Sprinkle on sage, parsley, and salt and pepper to taste.

5. Toss together over low heat for ½ minute more and serve immediately.

Formaggio Asiago e Mele

ASIAGO CHEESE AND APPLE · 96 CALORIES · 10.3 GR. CARBOHYDRATES

INGREDIENTS

½ oz. Asiago per serving
½ eating apple unpeeled per serving

Asiago is a cheese typical of Vicenza. It is made from partially skimmed cow's milk and is slightly sharp in taste.

METHOD

1. Cut cheese into thin slices and unpeeled apple into thin wedges. Alternate cheese and apple wedges in a pinwheel shape on each plate.

DINNER

Zucchine Ripiene

STUFFED ZUCCHINI · 50 CALORIES · 4.5 GR. CARBOHYDRATES

Spiedini di Gamberi Oreganato

BROCHETTES OF SHRIMP WITH OREGANO · 130 CALORIES · 5.0 GR. CARBOHYDRATES

Perle di Melone al Marsala

PEARLS OF MELON MARSALA · 48 CALORIES · 7.5 GR. CARBOHYDRATES

Total
Calories
111

Total
Carbohydrates
17.0 gr.

Zucchine Ripiene

STUFFED ZUCCHINI · 50 CALORIES · 4.5 GR. CARBOHYDRATES

INGREDIENTS

4 medium zucchini
1 Tb minced shallots or scallions
2 tsp minced garlic
1½ tsp oil
1 Tb minced parsley
1 Tb grated Parmesan cheese

METHOD

1. Wash zucchini thoroughly under cold running water. Slice off the stem ends and cut in half lengthwise.

2. Hollow out 4 of the halves, leaving a shell approximately ¼-inch thick to make "boats."

3. Grate the 2 remaining zucchini and the pulp from the "boats." Toss with 1 tsp salt and allow to drain for ½ hour in a strainer or collander.

4. Bring a large saucepan of lightly salted water to a boil. Drop in zucchini "boats" and blanch for 1 minute. Remove "boats" and pat dry with paper towels.

5. Taste grated zucchini and rinse with cold water if too salty. Then squeeze handfuls of zucchini to remove as much juice and water as possible.

6. Put 1 tsp olive oil in a non-stick skillet. Stir in minced shallots and grated zucchini. Sauté over medium heat for 1 minute, add garlic, parsley, and remaining ½ tsp oil. Continue to cook for 1 more minute.

7. Stir in ½ of grated Parmesan. Salt and pepper to taste.

8. Spoon zucchini into "boats." Sprinkle with remaining Parmesan and place under the broiler for a few seconds. Garnish "boats" with parsley and serve at once.

Spiedini di Gamberi Oreganato

BROCHETTES OF SHRIMP WITH OREGANO
130 CALORIES · 5.0 GR. CARBOHYDRATES

INGREDIENTS

8 metal brochette skewers
1 lb. raw shrimp, shelled and de-veined
1 Tb minced parsley
2 tsp fresh minced oregano or ½ tsp dry
1½ tsp lemon juice
1 Tb olive oil
Pepper to taste
1 Tb grated Parmesan cheese

Garnish:
1 lemon cut in 4 wedges
4 small bouquets of watercress or parsley
8 cherry tomatoes

METHOD

1. Preheat broiler to high.

2. Rinse shelled and de-veined shrimp in cold water and pat dry with paper towels.

3. Combine parsley, oregano, lemon juice, and olive oil in a small bowl.

4. Dip shrimp in herb-oil mixture and thread on skewers, making sure they are secure.

5. Sprinkle skewered shrimp with pepper and grated Parmesan. Broil for 2 to 3 minutes on each side or until firm and opaque. Do not overcook or shrimp will be rubbery.

6. Serve brochettes at once on warm plates. Garnish with lemon wedges and bouquets of watercress and cherry tomatoes.

Perle di Melone al Marsala

PEARLS OF MELON MARSALA · 48 CALORIES · 7.5 GR. CARBOHYDRATES

INGREDIENTS

1 ripe, flavorful honeydew melon or large cantaloupe, well chilled
2 tsp lemon juice
4 Tb Marsala
4 chilled wine glasses or cold soup or shrimp-cocktail icers

Garnish:
Fresh mint

METHOD

1. Cut open melon and remove seeds and stringy fibers.

2. Using a melon-ball scoop or a teaspoon, make 2 cups of melon balls.

3. Place melon balls in chilled glasses or icers. Sprinkle with lemon juice and Marsala. Garnish with mint.

4. Serve glasses on small dessert plates.

PIEDMONT

EMILIA

Genoa

Rapallo

Portofino

TUSCANY

San Remo

N

LIGURIA

LUNCHEON

Trenette al Pesto

NOODLES WITH PESTO SAUCE · 160 CALORIES · 20.1 GR. CARBOHYDRATES

Pesche Ripiene alla Ligure

STUFFED PEACHES LIGURIAN STYLE · 150 CALORIES · 25.0 GR. CARBOHYDRATES

Total
Calories
310

Total
Carbohydrates
45.1 gr.

Trenette al Pesto

NOODLES WITH PESTO SAUCE · 160 CALORIES · 20.1 GR. CARBOHYDRATES

INGREDIENTS

Pesto Sauce:
2 cups lightly packed raw spinach
½ cup lightly packed fresh basil leaves
2 tsp minced garlic
1 Tb olive oil
2 tsp low-fat ricotta cheese
1 Tb grated Parmesan cheese
⅛ tsp salt
Freshly ground pepper

5 oz. Trenette noodles if available. Otherwise use Fettuccine.
2 qt. water
2 tsp salt
2 tsp olive oil
4 tsp grated Parmesan cheese

Garnish:
Watercress and cherry tomatoes

METHOD

1. Place sauce ingredients, except salt and pepper, in a blender or food processor. Blend to achieve a smooth paste, then add salt and pepper to taste.

2. Bring water to a rolling boil, add salt, oil, and pasta. Cook for approximately 10 minutes, or until tender but still firm.

3. Pour pasta into a collander to drain, then into a mixing bowl. Toss pasta with ½ of pesto sauce.

4. Divide into 4 portions and top with remaining sauce and grated Parmesan. Garnish plates with bouquets of watercress and cherry tomatoes.

Pesche Ripiene alla Ligure

STUFFED PEACHES LIGURIAN STYLE · 150 CALORIES · 25.0 GR. CARBOHYDRATES

INGREDIENTS

5 ripe but unblemished peaches
¼ lemon
4 tsp raisins
Dash cinnamon and nutmeg
2 cups dry white wine
2 Tb honey
4 cloves
½ cinnamon stick

Garnish:
Fresh mint

METHOD

1. Preheat oven to 350°.

2. Drop peaches into boiling water for a few seconds to loosen skin, then peel and rub lightly with lemon.

3. Carefully cut peaches in half and remove pits.

4. Mash one peach and mix with raisins, cinnamon, and nutmeg.

5. Stuff mashed peach-and-raisin mixture into the hollow of a peach half and place the other half on top. Secure halves with kitchen string or toothpicks.

6. Combine wine, honey, cloves, and cinnamon stick in a saucepan. Bring to a boil and boil for 1 minute.

7. Place peaches in a deep-sided covered baking dish just large enough to hold them and pour over boiling wine mixture.

8. Bake peaches in the middle of preheated oven for 15 minutes or until just tender. Baste often if wine does not completely cover peaches.

9. Allow peaches to cool in wine and refrigerate in wine.

10. When ready to serve, carefully remove peaches with a slotted spoon and take off string or remove toothpicks.

11. Place each stuffed peach in a wine glass and garnish with a mint leaf. Pour chilled wine mixture around peach and serve.

DINNER

Zuppa di Pomodoro

CREAM OF TOMATO SOUP · 88 CALORIES · 14.6 GR. CARBOHYDRATES

Filetti di Pesce e Spinaci in Cartoccio
Spinaci alla Genovese

FISH FILETS AND SPINACH IN PAPER CASES
SPINACH GENOVESE STYLE
190 CALORIES · 6.8 GR. CARBOHYDRATES

Gelato di Fragole

STRAWBERRY ICE · 54 CALORIES · 13.5 GR. CARBOHYDRATES

Total
Calories
332

Total
Carbohydrates
34.9 gr.

Zuppa di Pomodoro

CREAM OF TOMATO SOUP · 88 CALORIES · 14.6 GR. CARBOHYDRATES

INGREDIENTS

1 tsp olive oil
1 cup chopped onion
1½ lb. peeled diced tomatoes
1½ tsp minced parsley
½ tsp fresh minced basil
⅛ tsp dry Italian Seasonings
Salt and pepper
½ cup plain low-fat yogurt
1½ cups chicken broth

Garnish:
1½ tsp minced fresh basil or 1½ tsp minced parsley

METHOD

1. Heat olive oil in a non-stick skillet. Add onions and sauté until golden.

2. Stir in diced tomatoes, honey, parsley, basil, Italian Seasonings, and salt and pepper to taste. Simmer, stirring occasionally, for 10 minutes.

3. Allow tomato mixture to cool, then purée.

4. Stir ½ cup yogurt into cooled purée. Then, stirring constantly, pour in hot chicken broth. Taste and adjust seasonings.

5. Stirring constantly, bring soup back almost to the boiling point. Do not boil or yogurt may curdle.

6. Sprinkle with fresh basil or parsley. Serve hot or chilled, depending on the season.

Filetti di Pesce e Spinaci in Cartoccio

FISH FILETS AND SPINACH IN PAPER CASES · 190 CALORIES · 6.8 GR. CARBOHYDRATES

INGREDIENTS

Prepare Spinach Genovese (see recipe following page)
4 6-oz. fish filets—sole, flounder, whiting, etc.
Salt and pepper to taste
4 8 × 10 inch rectangles of cooking parchment or heavy aluminum foil
1 Tb olive oil

2 Tb minced parsley
2 tsp snipped chives
1 tsp fresh minced basil or ¼ tsp dry Italian Seasonings
1 lemon cut into thin slices
1 large, pitted black olive (optional = 10 calories)

METHOD

1. Preheat oven to 375°.

2. Wash fish filets under cold running water, pat dry with paper towels, and sprinkle lightly with salt and pepper.

3. Fold parchment or foil in half lengthwise. Using the fold as the middle, cut out a half heart shape 7½ × 9½ inches. Unfold "heart" and oil its inner side lightly with olive oil. Prepare rest of parchment in same manner.

4. Combine remaining oil with herbs and spread on both sides of filets.

5. Spoon a bed of Spinach Genovese on one half of the oiled inside of "heart." Top spinach with a fish filet and top filet with a layer of lemon slices and thin olive rounds.

6. Fold the other half of "heart" over filet to envelop it. Then carefully fold the edges to seal the packets so that no steam or juice escapes during cooking.

7. Place packets on a lightly oiled cookie sheet and bake in the middle of preheated 375° oven for 15 minutes.

8. Serve filets in their packages.

Spinaci alla Genovese

SPINACH GENOVESE STYLE
55 CALORIES · 6.5 GR. CARBOHYDRATES · (INCLUDED IN FISH FILET RECIPE)

INGREDIENTS

1 lb. fresh spinach or 1 10-oz. package frozen spinach
1 oz. raisins and 1 cup hot water
2 tsp minced garlic
1 tsp butter and 1 tsp olive oil
Salt, pepper, and nutmeg to taste

METHOD

1. Remove large stems from fresh spinach and wash. Place in a saucepan with just the water clinging to the leaves. Cook, covered, until barely wilted, approximately 1 minute.

2. Squeeze spinach to remove as much water as possible. (My friend Natalie Dupree of Atlanta suggests pressing it between 2 plates.) Chop coarsely.

3. Soak raisins in hot water to soften, then drain.

4. Heat butter and oil in a non-stick skillet. Add minced garlic and sauté lightly, not allowing garlic to color.

5. Stir in spinach and raisins. Season to taste with salt, pepper, and nutmeg.

6. Simmer over low heat for 2 minutes to blend flavors.

7. Serve as an accompaniment to fish, fowl, or meat.

Gelato di Fragole

STRAWBERRY ICE · 54 CALORIES · 13.5 GR. CARBOHYDRATES

INGREDIENTS

1 pt. fresh ripe strawberries
3 Tb orange juice
2 Tb lemon juice
3 Tb honey
1 cup water

Garnish:
6 whole strawberries
Fresh mint

METHOD

1. Purée strawberries.

2. Stir in orange juice, lemon juice, honey, and water (if not sweet enough for your taste, add more honey: 61 calories·16.5 gr. carbohydrates per Tb).

3. Freeze ice in an ice-cream freezer, following your machine's directions for sherbets.

4. Serve ice in stemmed wine glasses. Garnish with whole strawberries and mint leaves.

Note: Off-season, frozen unsweetened strawberries may be used. Purée in a food processor with above ingredients, *except for water*. The result is an instant ice.

N

LOMBARDY

VENEZIA
EUGENEA

Piacenza

Parma
Modena
Ferrara

Bologna ◉ Ravenna

LIGURIA

Rimini

TUSCANY

THE
MARCHES

EMILIA ROMAGNA

LUNCHEON

Gnocchi Verdi con Salsa di Ricotta

SPINACH DUMPLINGS IN RICOTTA SAUCE · 173 CALORIES · 5.7 GR. CARBOHYDRATES

Fragole in Paniere di Arance

STRAWBERRIES IN ORANGE BASKETS · 80 CALORIES · 19.7 GR. CARBOHYDRATES

Total
Calories
153

Total
Carbohydrates
15.4 gr.

Gnocchi Verdi con Salsa di Ricotta

SPINACH DUMPLINGS IN RICOTTA SAUCE · 173 CALORIES · 5.7 GR. CARBOHYDRATES

INGREDIENTS

1 lb. fresh spinach or 1 10-oz. package chopped frozen
6 Tb whole milk ricotta
1 tsp minced garlic
½ tsp salt
1 egg yolk
2 Tb grated Romano cheese
Nutmeg and pepper to taste
4 qt. water and 1 Tb salt
2 egg whites
2 teaspoons

Ricotta Sauce:
½ cup part-skim ricotta
2 Tb grated Romano cheese
1 egg yolk
3 or 4 Tb hot water
Salt, pepper, and nutmeg to taste

Garnish:
4 tsp grated Romano cheese
4 cherry tomatoes
4 small bouquets of parsley

METHOD

1. If using fresh spinach, wash thoroughly and remove large stems. Place in a heavy covered saucepan with only the water clinging to leaves from washing. Cook covered over medium heat until just wilted, approximately 1 minute. Heat frozen spinach and 1 Tb of water until just defrosted.

2. Squeeze as much moisture out of spinach as possible. (See Step 2 Spinaci alla Genovese, p. 55.)

3. Chop spinach and scrape into a medium-size mixing bowl. Add ricotta, garlic, salt, egg yolk, 2 Tb grated Romano, nutmeg and pepper to taste. Mix thoroughly.

4. Start to heat salted water in a large saucepan or Dutch oven.

5. Beat egg whites until stiff but not dry. Fold into spinach mixture, ½ at a time, using a wooden or plastic spatula.

6. The salted water, once heated, should be maintained at the barest simmer for poaching. Do not let it come to a boil or the gnocchi may disintegrate.

7. Dip a spoon into simmering water, then dip out a rounded mass of spinach mixture. Transfer the spoon to your left hand and, using the inverted bowl of the second wet spoon, form the mixture into an egg-shaped gnocchi.

8. Use the second spoon to gently slip the gnocchi into the simmering water. Continue in the same fashion to rapidly form 3 or 4 more gnocchi.

9. After 2 minutes, gently turn gnocchi over with a slotted spoon and cook for 2 more minutes, trying to keep track of which is which. Do not be concerned if they do not keep a perfect egg shape, as they can be re-formed after poaching.

10. Carefully remove gnocchi with a slotted spoon and place on a linen towel or paper towels to drain and cool. Use a teaspoon to gently re-form egg shape.

11. Continue to make batches of gnocchi until all spinach mixture has been used. This amount makes approximately 32 gnocchi. Gnocchi can be made up to 1 day in advance if they are stored in lightly buttered baking dish, covered with waxed paper and aluminum foil, and refrigerated. Remove paper before baking.

12. When ready to serve, preheat oven to 350°. Cover with aluminum foil and heat for 10 minutes.

13. While gnocchi are heating, combine ricotta, Romano cheese, and an egg yolk in the top of a double boiler or in a heavy-bottomed saucepan. Heat, stirring with a wire whisk until hot, but do not allow to boil. Season with salt, pepper, and nutmeg to taste.

14. When gnocchi are hot, divide them into 4 portions, spoon over hot sauce, sprinkle with grated Romano, and more pepper and nutmeg to taste.

15. Garnish plates with cherry tomatoes and parsley, and serve.

Fragole in Paniere di Arance

STRAWBERRIES IN ORANGE BASKETS · 80 CALORIES · 19.7 GR. CARBOHYDRATES

INGREDIENTS

4 unblemished oranges
2 cups fresh strawberries
1 Tb honey

Garnish:
Fresh mint

METHOD

1. Using a small, sharp knife to cut and a grapefruit spoon to hollow, make orange baskets, following steps in the diagrams.

2. Wash strawberries and cut in half.

3. Squeeze orange pulp to remove juice. Mix juice with honey and add to strawberries. Refrigerate for at least ½ hour.

4. Fill baskets with chilled berries and orange-juice mixture. Serve baskets on beds of fresh mint.

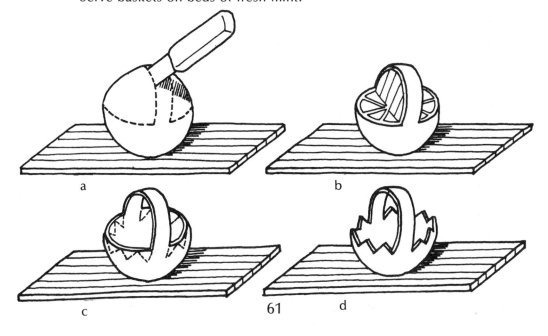

a

b

c

d

DINNER

Zuppa alla Modenese

SPINACH SOUP MODENESE STYLE · 102 CALORIES · 11.3 GR. CARBOHYDRATES

Petti di Pollo al Marsala

BREAST OF CHICKEN MARSALA · 205 CALORIES · 5.3 GR. CARBOHYDRATES

Mele alla Francese

APPLE SOUFFLÉ · 106 CALORIES · 16.3 GR. CARBOHYDRATES

Total
Calories
413

Total
Carbohydrates
32.9 gr.

Zuppa alla Modenese

SPINACH SOUP MODENESE STYLE · 102 CALORIES · 11.3 GR. CARBOHYDRATES

INGREDIENTS

1 1-lb. package fresh spinach or 1 package frozen chopped
1 tsp minced garlic
2 tsp butter
Salt, pepper, and nutmeg to taste
1 Tb grated Parmesan cheese
2 beaten egg yolks
3 cups beef broth
2 slices diet bread
2 tsp grated Parmesan cheese

METHOD

1. Wash spinach and remove large stems. Place in a heavy saucepan. Cover and cook with just the water on leaves until wilted (approximately 1 minute over medium heat).

2. If using frozen spinach, place still frozen in saucepan. Separate with fork, and cook until just defrosted.

3. Squeeze as much water as possible out of spinach. Purée it along with 1 tsp of minced garlic.

4. Melt butter in a non-stick skillet and add spinach purée. Cook slowly for 1 minute, stirring often. Stir in 1 Tb grated Parmesan, egg yolks, salt, pepper, and nutmeg to taste.

5. Bring beef broth to a boil and gradually pour into spinach mixture, stirring constantly.

6. Return soup to saucepan and return to a boil, stirring often. Spinach and egg mixture should curdle.

7. With a biscuit cutter, cut 4 rounds out of diet bread. Sprinkle rounds with grated Parmesan and place under a preheated broiler for a few seconds, until lightly toasted.

8. Spoon soup into consommé cups and float a toast round in each cup.

Petti di Pollo al Marsala

BREAST OF CHICKEN MARSALA · 205 CALORIES · 5.3 GR. CARBOHYDRATES

INGREDIENTS

4 boned ½ chicken breasts
4 large white mushrooms
1 tsp butter
Salt, pepper, and a few drops of lemon juice
3 Tb Marsala
1 Tb water
3 Tb beef broth
2 tsp grated Parmesan cheese
2 Tb chopped parsley

Garnish:
4 small bouquets of watercress
4 lemon wedges

METHOD

1. Sprinkle chicken breasts lightly with salt and pepper. Place between two pieces of waxed paper and pound until thin.

2. Trim the tips off stems of mushrooms and slice vertically into thin umbrella shapes.

3. Melt butter in a non-stick skillet. Add mushrooms, sprinkle lightly with salt, pepper, and a few drops of lemon juice.

4. Sauté mushrooms lightly. Remove with a slotted spoon and reserve in a warm place.

5. Place chicken breasts in skillet and cook over medium heat until lightly browned on both sides. Remove chicken to warm dish.

6. Add Marsala, water, and stock to skillet. Scrape the bottom of skillet with a wooden spatula to incorporate the cooking juices. This process is called deglazing.

7. Return chicken to skillet. Sprinkle with grated Parmesan and spoon pan juices over them. Reduce heat and cover skillet. Simmer for approximately 5 minutes or until pan juices have reduced to 5 Tb.

8. Put a layer of mushroom slices on top of each chicken breast. Spoon over sauce and sprinkle with parsley. Garnish plates with small bouquets of watercress and lemon wedges.

Mele alla Francese

APPLE SOUFFLÉ · 106 CALORIES · 16.3 GR. CARBOHYDRATES

INGREDIENTS

4 large unblemished cooking/eating apples
½ lemon
1½ cups unsweetened applesauce
1 Tb honey
Cinnamon and nutmeg to taste

1 Tb raisins
3 Tb applejack or Calvados (optional)
2 egg whites and a pinch of salt
A light sprinkling of confectioners' sugar

METHOD

1. Preheat oven to 375°.

2. If necessary, cut a thin slice off the bottom of each apple so it will stand straight.

3. Cut a ½-inch slice off the top of apples.

4. Using a small sharp knife and a grapefruit spoon, hollow out apples, leaving a shell ¼ inch thick.

5. Rub interior and top edges of apple shells with lemon to keep them from discoloring.

6. Combine applesauce, honey, cinnamon, nutmeg, raisins, and two tsp applejack in a heavy-bottomed saucepan. Heat, stirring often until hot but not boiling.

7. Beat egg whites and pinch of salt until stiff but not dry.

8. Pour hot applesauce into a medium-size mixing bowl. Add ½ of egg whites and fold in with a rubber or wooden spatula.

9. Add remaining egg whites and fold in very lightly.

10. Sprinkle the inside of apple shells lightly with cinnamon and nutmeg.

11. Place apple shells in a lightly buttered baking dish and carefully fill with soufflé mixture doming the top.

12. Bake in the center of preheated 375° oven for 15 to 17 minutes or until soufflés have risen and are very lightly browned on top.

13. If you plan to flame the soufflés, heat remaining applejack until warm in a small saucepan.

14. Remove soufflés from oven and sprinkle with confectioners' sugar.

15. Using a long match, light applejack and pour over soufflés. Serve at once.

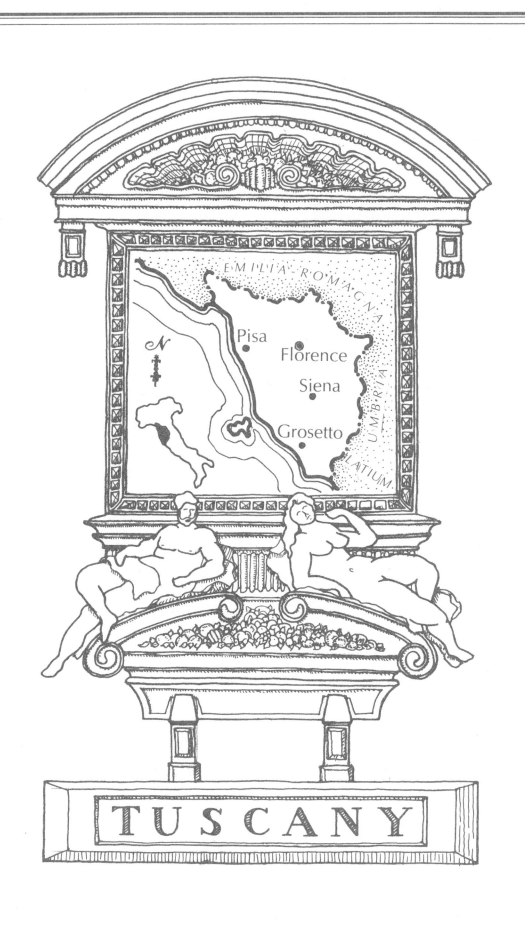

EMILIA·ROMAGNA

Pisa

Florence

Siena

Grosetto

U·M·B·R·I·A

LATIUM

N

TUSCANY

LUNCHEON

Insalata di Fagiolini e Cipolle

GREEN BEAN AND ONION SALAD · 78 CALORIES · 6.3 GR. CARBOHYDRATES

Frittata di Tonno

TUNA OMELETTE WITH YOGURT SAUCE · 132 CALORIES · 2.1 GR. CARBOHYDRATES

Budino di Ricotta

RICOTTA PUDDING · 128 CALORIES · 7.8 GR. CARBOHYDRATES

Total
Calories
338

Total
Carbohydrates
16.2 gr.

Insalata di Fagiolini e Cipolle

GREEN BEAN AND ONION SALAD · 78 CALORIES · 6.3 GR. CARBOHYDRATES

INGREDIENTS

⅔ lb. fresh green beans
2 qt. water
2 tsp salt
1 red bell pepper, long, round, and narrow in form if possible
1 large or 2 small green onions (scallions)

1½ Tb olive oil
2 tsp wine vinegar
Salt and pepper to taste
4 attractive lettuce leaves—romaine, Boston, or Bibb

METHOD

1. Wash all vegetables under cold running water.

2. Remove strings from beans.

3. Bring 1 qt. of lightly salted water to a rolling boil. Add beans and cook for not more than 1 minute. Beans should still be crisp.

4. Drain beans and refresh under cold running water to preserve color.

5. Core bell pepper and cut into rings ⅛ inch wide.

6. Slice green onions into thin rings. You should have about 2 Tb.

7. Place well-drained beans in a bowl and add chopped onion, olive oil, and vinegar. Toss together and sprinkle on salt and freshly ground pepper to taste.

8. Marinate beans for at least 15 minutes.

9. When ready to assemble, remove beans from the bowl and form 4 bundles.

10. Slip a pepper ring around the center of each bundle and place bundles on chilled salad plates covered with lettuce leaves.

11. Sprinkle onion and any remaining dressing over bundles and serve.

Frittata di Tonno

TUNA OMELETTE WITH YOGURT SAUCE · 132 CALORIES · 2.1 GR. CARBOHYDRATES

INGREDIENTS

5 eggs
3½-oz. can tuna packed in water
1½ tsp snipped chives (fresh or freeze-dried)
1 tsp fresh minced basil or ¼ tsp dry
1½ tsp minced parsley
½ tsp minced fresh mint or ⅛ tsp dry
1½ tsp lemon juice
⅛ tsp pepper
2 tsp grated Parmesan cheese

Yogurt Sauce:
5 Tb low-fat plain yogurt
½ tsp snipped chives
1 tsp minced parsley

METHOD

1. Beat eggs until well mixed.

2. Stir in drained flaked tuna, herbs, lemon juice, and pepper.

3. Pour mixture into a slightly preheated, non-stick skillet approximately 8 inches in diameter. Stir lightly once and cook over medium heat.

4. When edges begin to cook, lift them to allow the liquid egg to run under.

5. When no liquid remains on top, hold a plate firmly over the top of the skillet while inverting skillet with the other hand. This will leave the omelette on the plate. Then carefully slip the omelette, cooked side up, back into the skillet to brown lightly the other side.

6. Divide omelette into four wedges and serve topped with yogurt sauce.

69

Budino di Ricotta

RICOTTA PUDDING · 128 CALORIES · 7.8 GR. CARBOHYDRATES

INGREDIENTS

1 cup whole-milk ricotta
1 Tb honey
¼ tsp vanilla
2 egg whites
Pinch of salt
Cinnamon to taste
¼ cup fresh strawberries or raspberries (optional garnish)

METHOD

1. Combine ricotta, honey, and vanilla in a small heavy-bottomed saucepan or double boiler.

2. Beat 2 egg whites and a pinch of salt until stiff, but not dry.

3. Heat ricotta mixture, stirring with a wire whisk until hot but not yet simmering.

4. Pour ricotta mixture into a medium-size mixing bowl and carefully fold in the egg whites one half at a time, using a rubber or wooden spatula.

5. Spoon pudding into 4 wine glasses or pudding dishes. Sprinkle with cinnamon.

6. Chill pudding uncovered in refrigerator until ready to serve. Garnish with fresh berries.

Note: Pudding may begin to separate if made more than a few hours in advance.

DINNER

Tagliatelle con Salsa di Broccoli

NOODLES WITH BROCCOLI SAUCE · 240 CALORIES · 44.3 GR. CARBOHYDRATES

Bistecca alla Fiorentina

BEEFSTEAK FLORENTINE · 320 CALORIES · 4.1 GR. CARBOHYDRATES

Gelato di Melone

MELON ICE · 24 CALORIES · 7.4 GR. CARBOHYDRATES

*Total
Calories
584*

*Total
Carbohydrates
55.8 gr.*

Tagliatelle con Salsa di Broccoli

NOODLES WITH BROCCOLI SAUCE · 240 CALORIES · 44.3 GR. CARBOHYDRATES

INGREDIENTS

1 medium bunch of broccoli. Divide into bite-size flowerets, trim the woody end off stems, peel stems, and cut into 1-inch lengths. You should have 3 cups of flowerets, 1⅓ cup stems.
3 cups lightly salted water
1 tsp minced garlic
1 tsp olive oil

3 tsp fresh chopped basil or ¾ tsp dry sweet basil
1 Tb low-fat ricotta cheese
¼ tsp salt, ⅛ tsp pepper
Pinch nutmeg (optional)
8 oz. Tagliatelle or Fettuccini noodles
2 qt. water and 2 tsp salt
4 tsp grated Parmesan cheese

METHOD

Sauce and Garnish:

1. Bring salted water to a rapid boil, add broccoli stems, and cook uncovered at slow boil for 3 minutes or until just tender.

2. In a non-stick skillet, cook minced garlic in olive oil over low heat until slightly softened, but not colored. Stir often.

3. Reserving cooking water, remove the stems with a slotted spoon, and add to garlic and oil in skillet. Cover and cook over low heat for 3 minutes. If mixture seems too dry, add 1 Tb of cooking water.

4. Bring the poaching liquid back to a boil and add broccoli flowerets. Boil slowly uncovered for 1 minute or until barely cooked. Remove 1⅓ cups flowerets with slotted spoon, refresh in cold water to preserve fresh color, drain, and set aside for garnish.

5. Remove remaining flowerets from poaching liquid and add to stems and garlic in skillet. Stir together, cook slowly for 2 more minutes.

6. Allow poaching liquid to boil down to ½ cup.

7. Purée stems, flowerets, and ricotta. Gradually add poaching liquid until sauce reaches desired thickness. Add salt and pepper and optional nutmeg to taste.

8. Keep sauce warm in a double boiler until ready to use. 1 minute before serving, plunge a strainer filled with garnish flowerets into boiling pasta water for a few seconds to heat slightly.

Pasta:

1. Bring 2 qt. salted water to a rolling boil in a large saucepan. Add 2 tsp salt and stir in pasta. Cook for 8 to 10 minutes until tender but not mushy. (The longer pasta cooks, the fewer calories it has.)

2. Drain pasta. Put into a mixing bowl and toss with ½ of sauce. Divide into 4 portions. Sprinkle each one with ⅓ cup broccoli flowerets. Top with more sauce and a light sprinkling of grated Parmesan cheese. Serve at once.

Bistecca alla Fiorentina

BEEFSTEAK FLORENTINE · 320 CALORIES · 4.1 GR. CARBOHYDRATES

INGREDIENTS

1 lb. porterhouse or sirloin steak at least 1 inch thick. Trim off fat.

Marinade:
1 tsp olive oil
½ tsp lemon juice
½ tsp wine vinegar
1 tsp minced parsley
½ tsp fresh minced oregano or ⅛ tsp dry
½ tsp minced garlic
salt and pepper to taste

Garnish:
4 lemon wedges
2 medium tomatoes
2 tsp minced fresh basil
1 tsp olive oil
½ tsp red wine vinegar

METHOD

1. Combine marinade ingredients, spread over steak, and marinate in the refrigerator for 2 hours.

2. Grill over charcoal if possible or in a broiler that has been preheated for 10 minutes. This steak is traditionally served rare. Broil for 3 to 4 minutes on each side.

3. Slice steak on a slight angle into slices ½ inch thick.

4. Divide slices into 4 portions. Serve with lemon wedges and garnish plates with tomato slices. Sprinkle fresh basil and a few drops of vinegar and oil over tomatoes.

73

Gelato di Melone

MELON ICE · 24 CALORIES · 7.4 GR. CARBOHYDRATES · SERVES 6

INGREDIENTS

2 cups puréed cantaloupe or honeydew melon (melon should be very ripe and flavorful)
Juice of 1 lemon
1 Tb honey
1 cup water

Garnish:
Bite-size wedges of melon marinated in lemon juice or in Port or Marsala wine

METHOD

1. Combine melon purée, water, lemon juice, and honey. Add more honey if necessary (61 calories · 165 gr. carbohydrates per tablespoon).

2. Freeze sherbet in an ice-cream freezer, following the directions of your machine, or pour mixture into ice trays that have been washed in scalding water and rinsed with baking soda and cold water to remove any odors.

3. If using the ice-tray method, fill trays only ⅔ full and stir sherbet with a fork or whisk 2 or 3 times during the freezing process to give it a lighter, fluffier texture.

4. Spoon sherbet into stemmed wine glasses and garnish with melon wedges and fresh mint.

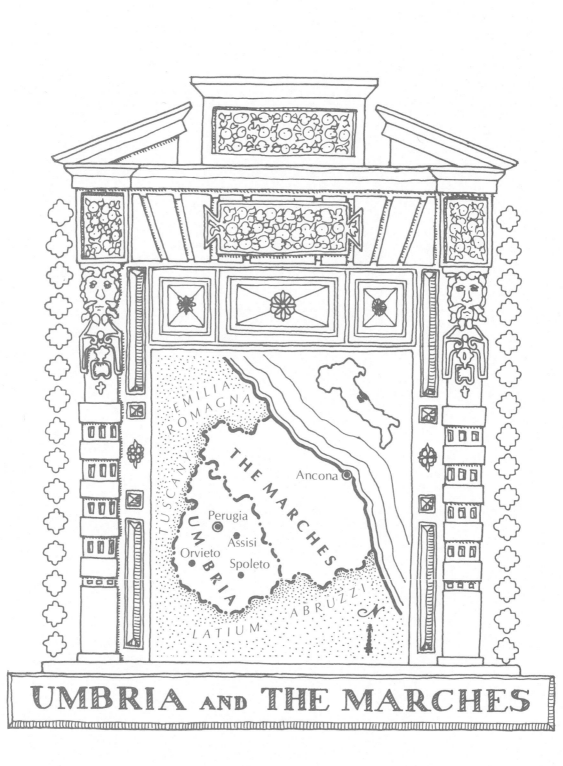

UMBRIA and THE MARCHES

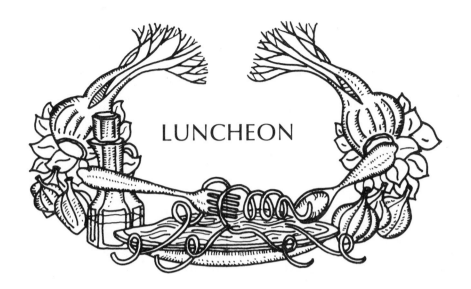

LUNCHEON

Insalata di Finocchio e Rucola

FENNEL AND ARUGULA SALAD · 83 CALORIES · 7.5 GR. CARBOHYDRATES

Spaghetti Aglio ed Olio

SPAGHETTI WITH OIL, GARLIC, AND GINGER · 273 CALORIES · 22.0 GR. CARBOHYDRATES

Zabaione Semi Freddo

FROZEN WINE CUSTARD · 112 Calories · 0.4 GR. CARBOHYDRATES

Total Calories 468

Total Carbohydrates 29.9 gr.

Insalata di Finocchio e Rucola

FENNEL AND ARUGULA SALAD · 83 CALORIES · 7.5 GR. CARBOHYDRATES

INGREDIENTS

2 large bulbs fresh fennel
1½ cup arugula leaves, washed and dried with paper towels
1½ Tb olive oil
1¼ tsp wine vinegar
Salt and freshly ground pepper to taste

Note: If fennel is not available, celery may be substituted and a few drops of anise-flavored liqueur added to dressing.

METHOD

1. Cut off stalks of fennel and reserve for Pollo alla Perugina (page 81).

2. Peel off the stringy outside of the bulb with a vegetable peeler or sharp knife.

3. Cut the bulb in quarters and core. Then slice quarters into thin crescents. Wash in cold water and dry with paper towels.

4. Combine arugula and fennel crescents in a bowl and add oil, vinegar, and salt and pepper to taste.

5. Toss gently to coat all ingredients lightly. Taste and adjust seasonings.

6. Arrange salad attractively on 4 chilled salad plates.

Spaghetti Aglio ed Olio

SPAGHETTI WITH OIL, GARLIC, AND GINGER · 273 CALORIES · 22.0 GR. CARBOHYDRATES

INGREDIENTS

8 oz. dry spaghetti
4 qt. water
1 Tb salt
1 Tb olive oil

Sauce:
2 Tb olive oil
2 tsp minced ginger root
2 tsp minced garlic
2 Tb minced parsley

METHOD

1. Bring 4 qt. water to a rolling boil. Stir in 1 Tb salt and spaghetti. After 6 minutes, add 1 Tb oil to the cooking water and continue cooking for approximately 2 minutes more, or until spaghetti is just tender.

2. While spaghetti is cooking, heat oil to just below a boil. Stir in ginger, garlic, and parsley and remove from heat.

3. Drain spaghetti and toss with sauce. Serve at once.

Zabaione Semi Freddo

FROZEN WINE CUSTARD · 112 CALORIES · 7.4 GR. CARBOHYDRATES

INGREDIENTS

2 egg yolks
2 Tb Marsala
2 tsp honey
1 envelope diet whipped-topping mix

½ tsp Marsala
½ cup low-fat milk
Cinnamon or nutmeg to taste

METHOD

1. Beat egg yolks, Marsala, and honey until light and fluffy.

2. Whip the topping mix with ½ tsp Marsala and milk until it stands in peaks.

3. Pour egg-yolk mixture into the top of a double boiler and whip constantly with a whisk over boiling water until it doubles in volume.

4. Carefully fold yolk mixture into the whipped topping.

5. Spoon into stemmed glasses, sprinkle lightly with cinnamon or nutmeg, and place in freezer for at least one hour before serving.

DINNER

Pollo alla Perugina

ROAST CHICKEN WITH FENNEL · 215 CALORIES · 0.1 GR. CARBOHYDRATES

Pomodori al Forno

BAKED TOMATO HALVES · 38 CALORIES · 5.3 GR. CARBOHYDRATES

Crespelle di Ciliege

CHERRY CREPES · 142 CALORIES · 28.0 GR. CARBOHYDRATES

Total Calories
395

Total Carbohydrates
33.4 gr.

Pollo alla Perugina

ROAST CHICKEN WITH FENNEL · 215 CALORIES · 0.1 GR. CARBOHYDRATES

INGREDIENTS

1 small roasting chicken (approximately
 2½ lb.)
1½ tsp olive oil
1 Tb minced parsley
1½ tsp minced garlic
½ tsp grated lemon rind

1 Tb minced fresh fennel or ½ tsp fennel seeds
Salt and pepper

Garnish:
Parsley
Lemon wedges

METHOD

1. Preheat oven to 400°.

2. Remove any loose fat from the inside of the chicken and wash chicken under cold running water. Pat it dry, inside and out, with paper towels.

3. *Optional but Advisable:* When cooking any whole fowl, remove the wishbone to simplify slicing.

a. Turn back the skin around the neck opening and feel with your fingers to find the wishbone of the chicken. It is very near the surface of the flesh and frames the neck opening like an arch.

b. With a small, sharp knife, cut around the outline of the wishbone. Then insert blade behind the bone and cut down to free the two sides of the bone at their base. Remove bone.

4. In a small bowl, combine oil, parsley, garlic, lemon rind, and fennel.

5. Sprinkle chicken inside and out with salt and pepper.

6. Carefully run your hand between the skin and the flesh of the chicken, starting at the base of the breast. Separate the skin from the flesh over as much of the chicken as possible, except for the area around the neck opening.

7. With your hand or a rubber spatula, spread a layer of the oil-herb mixture between skin and flesh.

8. Truss chicken and set in a lightly oiled roasting pan.

9. Place chicken in the middle of preheated 400° oven for 10 minutes, then turn it on one side for 5 minutes and on the other side for 5 more minutes to brown evenly.

10. Lower oven to 350° and cook the chicken, breast up, for approximately 30 minutes more, or until leg moves easily in its socket and the juice from the chicken is clear with no trace of red in it.

11. Carve chicken into 4 servings.

12. Serve chicken with baked tomato halves and garnish plates with parsley and lemon wedges.

Pomodori al Forno

BAKED TOMATO HALVES · 38 CALORIES · 5.3 GR. CARBOHYDRATES

INGREDIENTS

2 large firm ripe tomatoes
2 tsp olive oil
1½ tsp minced parsley
1½ tsp minced garlic
1 tsp minced fresh mint or ¼ tsp mint flakes
2 tsp grated Parmesan cheese
Salt and pepper to taste

METHOD

1. Preheat oven to 350°.

2. Cut tomatoes in half and place in an oiled baking dish, cut sides up.

3. Combine oil, parsley, garlic, and mint in a small bowl. Divide into 4 portions and spread over tomato halves.

4. Sprinkle tomatoes with Parmesan and a bit of salt and pepper.

5. Bake in 350° oven for approximately 15 minutes.

Crespelle di Ciliege

CHERRY CREPES · 142 CALORIES · 28.0 GR. CARBOHYDRATES

INGREDIENTS

Cherries in Wine Syrup:
1 cup red wine
3 Tb honey
The zest (outer peel) of ⅛ lemon
2 cloves
⅛ tsp cinnamon or to taste
2 cups ripe sour cherries or 1 16-oz. can tart cherries in water well drained

½ tsp cornstarch (optional)
A light sprinkling of confectioners' sugar

Flourless Crepe Batter:
1 egg and 1 egg white
3 Tb water
Dash cinnamon and dash nutmeg

METHOD

1. Place wine, honey, lemon zest, cloves, and cinnamon in a heavy-bottomed saucepan. Stir with a wire whisk to incorporate honey thoroughly. Bring mixture to a boil.

2. If using fresh cherries, add them to wine and simmer for 20 minutes or until tender. If using canned cherries, boil wine down to ½ cup, add cherries, and simmer for 3 or 4 minutes.

3. Allow cherries to cool in the wine. Then remove cloves and lemon zest.

4. If a thicker syrup is desired, remove cherries from wine with a slotted spoon and add cornstarch to wine. Heat, stirring with a wire whisk until slightly thickened, then return cherries to wine syrup and set aside until ready to assemble crepes.

5. Whisk egg, egg white, water, nutmeg, and cinnamon together in a small mixing bowl.

6. Preheat a small non-stick skillet (6 inches in diameter) over a medium flame and spoon in 2 to 3 Tb of batter, turning skillet to cover the bottom evenly.

7. Return to medium heat and cook until the top is dry and the bottom lightly browned.

8. Turn crepe out onto a plate and make three more crepes in the same way (can be made ahead to this point a few hours in advance and stored between two plates).

9. When ready to assemble crepes, preheat oven to 350°.

10. Place crepes in a baking dish, browned side down. Spoon half of cherry mixture onto one side and fold over the other.

11. Heat crepes in a preheated oven for a few minutes and at the same time heat remaining cherry mixture.

12. Serve crepes topped with cherry mixture.

TUSCANY

UMBRIA

ABRUZZI

N

Viterbo

Tivoli

Rome

Frascati

Ostia

Anzio

LATIUM

LUNCHEON

Pomodori Ripieni Primavera

TOMATOES STUFFED WITH RICE AND SPRING VEGETABLES
156 CALORIES · 31.8 GR. CARBOHYDRATES

Melone Cantalupo

CANTALOUPE · 50 CALORIES · 13.5 GR. CARBOHYDRATES

Total
Calories
206

Total
Carbohydrates
45.3 gr.

Pomodori Ripieni Primavera

TOMATOES STUFFED WITH RICE AND SPRING VEGETABLES
156 CALORIES · 31.8 GR. CARBOHYDRATES

INGREDIENTS

1⅓ cup water
½ tsp salt
⅔ cup converted rice
⅛ tsp dry Italian Seasonings
4 large firm tomatoes
¼ lb. green beans
1 small zucchini

Salt and pepper
3 Tb grated Romano cheese
1 Tb minced parsley
2 tsp fresh minced mint

Garnish:
4 large mint leaves

METHOD

1. Bring water to a rolling boil. Add salt and stir in rice and Italian Seasonings. Cover and simmer over low heat for 20 minutes or until rice is tender and liquid absorbed.

2. While rice is cooking, cut a slice ¼ inch thick from the stem end of each tomato. Cut out the stem and reserve slices as "lids."

3. Hollow out tomatoes, seed and strain. Dice pulp and reserve.

4. Fill the bottom of a steamer with water and bring to a boil.

5. Thoroughly wash beans and zucchini under cold running water. Snap ends off beans to remove strings and cut into 1-inch lengths. Slice zucchini into rounds ⅛ inch thick, then halve the rounds to make half-moon shapes.

6. Sprinkle inside of tomato shells with salt and pepper. Invert shells and place in steamer basket with zucchini and beans. Cover and steam for 3 minutes. Remove tomato shells and zucchini, but continue to steam beans for 2 minutes more.

7. Toss rice, tomato pulp, zucchini, beans, minced parsley, mint, and 2 Tb Romano cheese together, season with salt and pepper to taste.

8. Fill tomatoes with rice mixture, sprinkle with remaining Romano, and replace lids. Stick a mint leaf in the stem hollow of each tomato and serve.

Melone Cantalupo

CANTALOUPE · 50 CALORIES · 13.5 GR. CARBOHYDRATES

INGREDIENTS

1 large cantaloupe, well chilled

Garnish:
4 wedges of lemon or lime.

METHOD

The cantaloupe we know today is a descendant of a melon grown by the ancient Romans. It gets its name because it was selectively cultivated and improved at Cantalupo, a Vatican property near Rome.

1. Cut cantaloupe in quarters. Seed.

2. Using a sharp knife, carefully cut between the rind and the flesh of the melon, removing the crescent of flesh in one piece.

3. Place flesh back on the rind and make horizontal cuts across the crescent to form bite-size pieces.

4. Place melon quarters on plates and carefully push cut pieces of melon in alternating directions so that the end result looks something like a boat with oars.

5. Garnish with lemon or lime wedges and fresh mint.

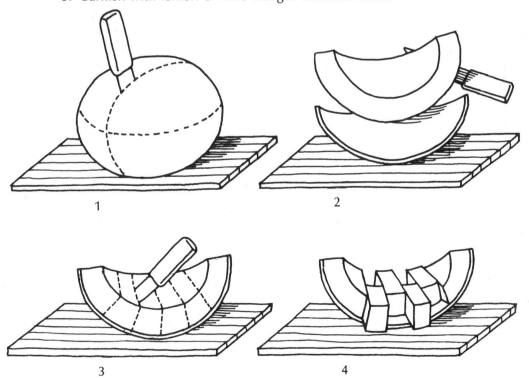

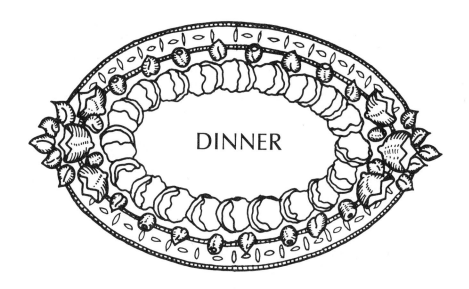

DINNER

Stracciatella

ROMAN CONSOMMÉ · 75 CALORIES · 2.5 GR. CARBOHYDRATES

Vitello Tonnato

COLD VEAL WITH TUNA FISH SAUCE · 357 CALORIES · 4.8 GR. CARBOHYDRATES

Mele al Vino Rosso

APPLES POACHED IN RED WINE · 150 CALORIES · 33.0 GR. CARBOHYDRATES

Total
Calories
582

Total
Carbohydrates
40.3 gr.

Stracciatella

ROMAN CONSOMMÉ · 75 CALORIES · 2.5 GR. CARBOHYDRATES

INGREDIENTS

4 cups strong, clear chicken broth (canned or homemade)
1½ tsp fresh minced oregano or ½ tsp dry
2 eggs
2 Tb minced parsley
1 Tb grated Romano cheese
2 Tb lemon juice
Pepper to taste

METHOD

1. Bring broth and oregano to a boil.

2. Beat eggs, parsley, cheese, and lemon juice together until yellow and frothy.

3. Add egg mixture to broth and stir lightly with a whisk to form "little rags." Add pepper to taste.

4. Serve at once.

Vitello Tonnato

COLD VEAL WITH TUNA FISH SAUCE · 357 CALORIES · 4.8 GR. CARBOHYDRATES

INGREDIENTS

1 lb. piece well-trimmed, boneless top round from the leg of veal
2 anchovy filets, cut into thirds
1 carrot
1 small onion
2 cloves
1 stalk celery
1 bay leaf
½ tsp salt or to taste
¼ tsp pepper or to taste
Cold water to cover

Tuna Sauce:
1 3½-oz. can tuna packed in oil, drained
1 hard-boiled egg yolk, reserve white for garnish

2 tsp chopped red onion
1 anchovy filet
1 Tb olive oil
2 tsp lemon juice
½ tsp capers
3 Tb low-fat yogurt

Garnish:
½ lemon thinly sliced
2 Tb thinly sliced red onion
1 Tb minced parsley
¼ tsp capers
1 hard-boiled egg white

METHOD

1. Sprinkle veal lightly with salt and pepper. Make incisions with a sharp knife and insert pieces of anchovy into the meat.

2. Tie veal with string so it will keep a neat, block-like shape.

3. Place a peeled halved carrot, 1 small onion stuck with 2 cloves, and a stalk of celery in a large saucepan.

4. Top with veal and add enough cold water to cover veal.

5. Add bay leaf, salt and pepper, bring to a boil, skimming off foam that rises to the top, then lower heat and simmer for 1 hour or until veal is tender. Allow veal to cool in cooking broth.

6. While veal is cooling, prepare tuna sauce. Combine tuna, egg yolk, onion, and anchovy filet in a blender or food processor and purée.

7. When purée is smooth, gradually add olive oil and then lemon juice and ¼ tsp capers as you continue to blend.

8. Scrape mixture into a mixing bowl. Stir in 3 Tb yogurt and ¼ tsp capers. Taste and, if necessary, add a bit of salt or pepper.

9. Remove cool veal to a carving board and cut into slices approximately ¼ inch thick.

10. Arrange slices on a small oval platter in an overlapping pattern and spoon over sauce so veal is completely covered.

11. Garnish platter with lemon slices, red onion slices, parsley, and capers. If you wish, decorative cut-outs of hard-boiled egg white can also be used.

12. Chill veal for at least 3 hours before serving.

90

Mele al Vino Rosso

APPLES POACHED IN RED WINE · 150 CALORIES · 33.0 GR. CARBOHYDRATES

INGREDIENTS

4 ripe firm cooking/eating apples
Acidulated water: 1 Tb lemon juice, 2 cups cold
    water
1½ cups full-bodied red wine
½ cup water

3 Tb honey
½ tsp cinnamon or 1 small cinnamon stick
¼ lemon
4 whole cloves
2 Tb unsweetened applesauce

METHOD

1. Core apples from the bottom, leaving the stem intact, then peel. If necessary, cut thin slice from bottom so they will stand.

2. Drop apples in acidulated water to prevent discoloring.

3. Place wine, water, honey, cinnamon, and nutmeg in a saucepan large enough to hold apples in one layer. Squeeze juice from ¼ lemon. Then stick cloves in lemon rind and add to the syrup mixture.

4. Boil over high heat for 2 minutes. Drop in drained apples and let the syrup return to a boil.

5. Turn down the heat and simmer uncovered for 15 minutes or until apples are easily pierced with a knife but still hold their shape.

6. If apples are not completely immersed in the syrup, turn them from time to time so they will color evenly.

7. Allow apples to cool in the syrup, continuing to turn them.

8. Remove apples carefully with a slotted spoon and place in a bowl.

9. Reduce syrup to one third of the original volume over high heat, then stir in applesauce.

10. Pour syrup over apples and chill.

11. Serve apples in individual compotes with syrup spooned over them.

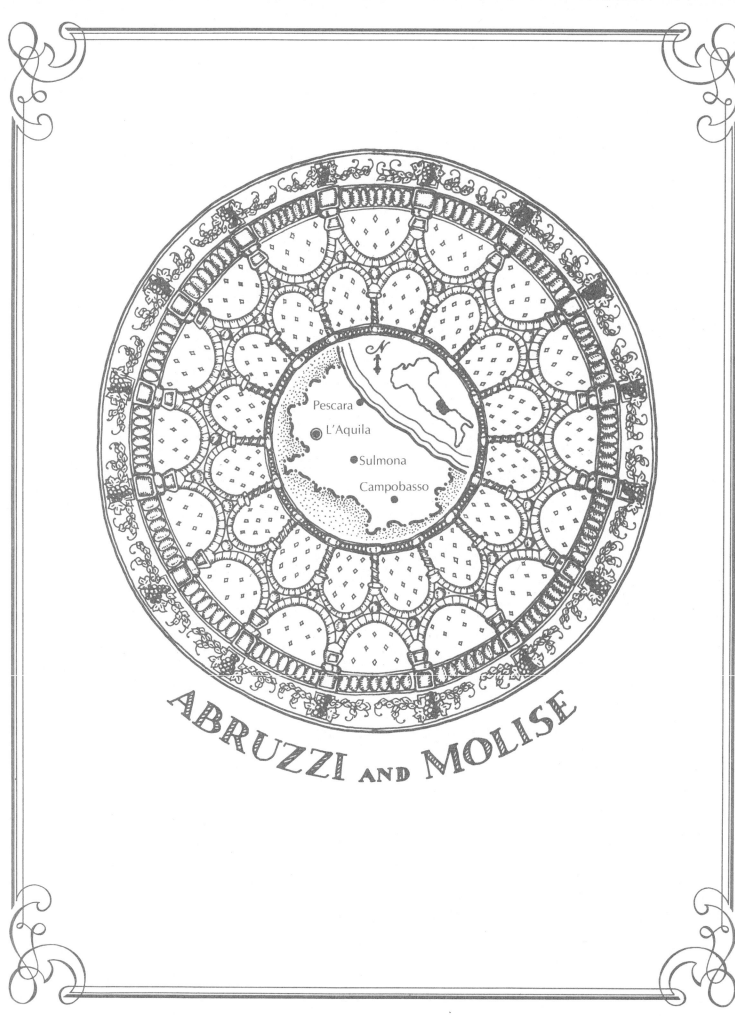

Pescara

L'Aquila

Sulmona

Campobasso

ABRUZZI AND MOLISE

LUNCHEON

Insalata di Crescione

WATERCRESS SALAD · 64 CALORIES · 2.8 GR. CARBOHYDRATES

Timballo di Pollo e Spinaci

CHICKEN AND SPINACH TORT · 235 CALORIES · 8.8 GR. CARBOHYDRATES

Formaggio Pecorino e Pere

PECORINO CHEESE AND PEAR · 107 CALORIES · 13.1 GR. CARBOHYDRATES

Total Calories 406

Total Carbohydrates 24.7 gr.

Insalata di Crescione

WATERCRESS SALAD · 64 CALORIES · 2.8 GR. CARBOHYDRATES

INGREDIENTS

½ lb. watercress
1 hard-boiled egg
1 scallion, thinly sliced
1½ tsp capers, drained
1 Tb olive oil
1 tsp wine vinegar or lemon juice
Salt and freshly ground pepper

METHOD

1. Wash watercress thoroughly, discarding thick stems. Dry with paper towels and break into bite-size pieces and place in a bowl.

2. Slice hard-boiled egg into rounds and add to watercress.

3. Add sliced scallion and capers to salad and top with olive oil.

4. Sprinkle salad with vinegar and salt and pepper to taste.

5. Toss gently, being careful not to break egg slices, and arrange attractively on 4 chilled salad plates.

Timballo di Pollo e Spinaci

CHICKEN AND SPINACH TORT · 235 CALORIES · 8.8 GR. CARBOHYDRATES

INGREDIENTS

Batter for flourless crepes (makes 6)
2 eggs
¼ cup plus 2 Tb cold water
⅛ tsp salt
1 Tb minced parsley
Pepper and nutmeg to taste

Spinach filling:
1 lb. fresh spinach or 1 10-oz. package chopped frozen
4 Tb low-fat ricotta cheese
½ tsp minced garlic
Salt, pepper, and nutmeg to taste
½ oz. low-fat Mozzarella cheese grated

Chicken Zucchini filling:
6 oz. shredded poached, or roasted, chicken breast

½ cup zucchini, sliced in rounds, then quartered
Fresh tomato sauce and 1½ tsp grated Parmesan cheese

Fresh Tomato Sauce:
1 tsp olive oil
3 Tb finely chopped onion
2 Tb minced parsley
1 lb. tomatoes peeled and diced
¼ tsp dry Italian Seasonings
A pinch of sugar
Salt and pepper to taste
1½ tsp grated Parmesan cheese
1½ tsp minced parsley

METHOD

1. Combine eggs, water, salt, parsley, pepper, and nutmeg and beat until well blended.

2. Preheat an 8-inch non-stick skillet slightly and pour in approximately 2 Tb of batter. Tip the skillet so the bottom is evenly coated.

3. Return skillet to heat for a few seconds. When the top is no longer moist and bottom is lightly browned, crepe is done. Turn finished crepe out onto dish and proceed until you have 6 crepes. Can be done ahead to this point, several hours in advance. When cool, cover crepes lightly with foil.

4. Place spinach in a saucepan with just the water from washing on the leaves. Cover and cook over low heat until just wilted, approximately 1 minute.

5. Squeeze as much water out of spinach as possible and chop and combine well with ricotta, garlic, salt, pepper, nutmeg, and Mozzarella. Spinach filling can be prepared several hours in advance and refrigerated.

6. Place olive oil in a large non-stick skillet. Add onion and cook over medium heat until softened, but not colored.

7. Stir in parsley, diced tomato, Italian Seasonings, sugar, salt, and pepper. Cover and simmer, stirring occasionally, for 15 minutes.

8. Toss ½ of tomato sauce with shredded chicken and zucchini. Reserve remaining sauce.

9. When ready to assemble timballo, preheat oven to 350°.

10. Place one crepe, brown side up, in a lightly oiled pie plate. Carefully spread ⅓ of spinach mixture on crepe.

11. Top with another crepe, brown side up, and cover with ½ of chicken-zucchini mixture. Continue in this fashion, alternating fillings until all crepes have been used.

12. Place timballo in the middle of preheated oven and bake for approximately 20 minutes, or until heated through.

13. Heat remaining tomato sauce and spoon on top of the timballo:

14. Sprinkle grated Parmesan cheese and parsley over the timballo. Cut into wedges and serve at once.

95

Formaggio Pecorino e Pere

PECORINO CHEESE AND PEAR · 107 CALORIES · 13.1 GR. CARBOHYDRATES

INGREDIENTS

½ oz. sharp Pecorino (Romano) cheese per serving
½ pear cored, but unpeeled, per serving

Pecorino cheese, though often used as grating cheese, is delicious as a table cheese as well. Aged for a minimum of eight months, it is pale yellow or white in color and pleasantly sharp in flavor.

METHOD

1. Arrange a slice of cheese and a half pear, skin side up, decoratively on each plate.

DINNER

Fettuccine in Salsa

FETTUCCINI WITH FRESH VEGETABLES · 157 CALORIES · 23.3 GR. CARBOHYDRATES

Bracioline d'Agnello

LAMB CHOPS · 140 CALORIES · 0.5 GR. CARBOHYDRATES

Granita di Caffe

COFFEE ICE · 62 CALORIES · 17.0 GR. CARBOHYDRATES

Total
Calories
359

Total
Carbohydrates
40.8 gr.

Fettuccine in Salsa

FETTUCCINE WITH FRESH VEGETABLES · 157 CALORIES · 23.3 GR. CARBOHYDRATES

INGREDIENTS

4 oz. dry Fettuccini noodles
3 qt. boiling water
1 Tb salt
1 cup zucchini cut into rounds ⅛ inch thick, then quartered
1 cup peeled diced tomatoes
1½ Tb minced parsley
1½ tsp fresh chopped mint
½ tsp minced garlic
6 paper-thin slices red onion divided into rings
1 Tb olive oil
1½ tsp vinegar
Salt and pepper

METHOD

1. Cook pasta in boiling salted water until just tender.

2. While pasta is cooking, combine zucchini, diced tomato, on-ion, parsley, mint, garlic, oil, and vinegar. Add salt and pepper to taste.

3. Drain pasta and quickly toss with sauce. Serve at once.

Bracioline d'Agnello

LAMB CHOPS · 140 CALORIES · 0.5 GR. CARBOHYDRATES

INGREDIENTS

⅛ cup water
5 minced fresh sage leaves or ¼ tsp dry sage
4 6-oz. lamb chops weighed uncooked with
    bone. Trim off as much fat as possible.
Salt and pepper
½ cup dry white wine

Garnish:
1 lemon cut into wedges
4 bouquets watercress or parsley

METHOD

1. Combine water and sage. Dip chops just long enough to moisten them and to coat lightly with sage.

2. Brown chops for 3 minutes on each side in a preheated non-stick skillet. Then sprinkle lightly with salt and pepper.

3. Add wine to skillet and continue cooking until wine has evaporated and chops are tender, approximately 2 minutes.

4. Serve chops garnished with lemon wedges and watercress or parsley bouquets.

Granita di Caffe

COFFEE ICE · 62 CALORIES · 17.0 GR. CARBOHYDRATES

INGREDIENTS

8 Tb drip-grind coffee
3 cups water

4 Tb honey
Grated rind of 1 lemon

METHOD

1. Put coffee in coffee pot and add 3 cups boiling water.

2. Add honey.

3. Cover and let brew for 20 minutes.

4. Pour mixture through filter paper into freezer trays.

5. Place trays in freezer. Stir several times with a fork as the mixture is freezing to achieve a granular texture.

6. Spoon into wine glasses and sprinkle with lemon rind.

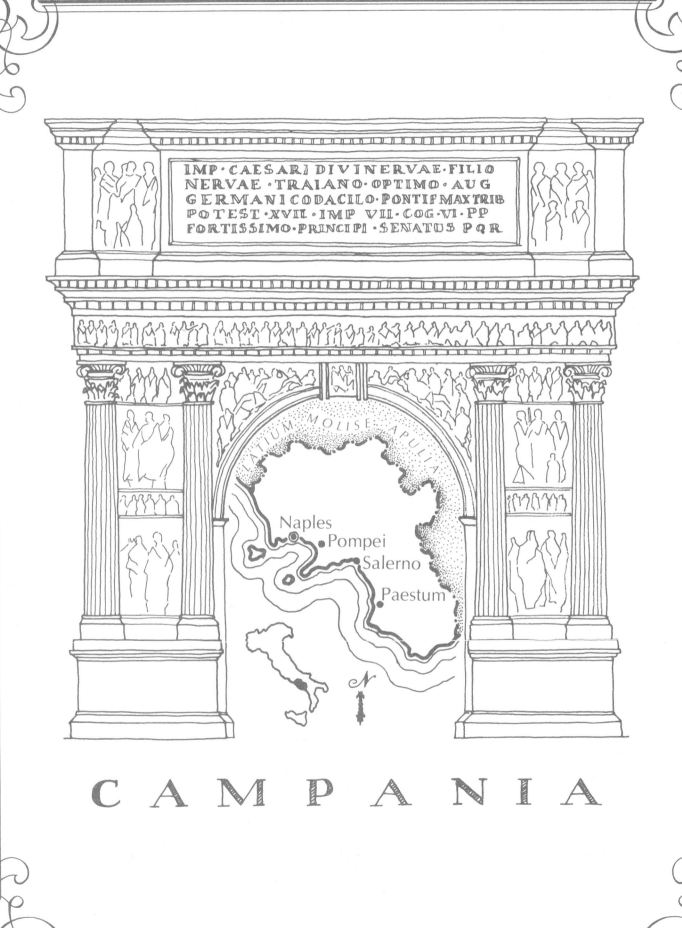

IMP · CAESARI DIVINERVAE · FILIO
NERVAE · TRAIANO · OPTIMO · AUG
GERMANICODACILO · PONTIFMAXTRIB
POTEST · XVII · IMP VII · COG · VI · PP
FORTISSIMO · PRINCIPI · SENATUS PQR

LATIUM · MOLISE · APULIA

Naples
Pompei
Salerno
Paestum

N

CAMPANIA

LUNCHEON

Insalata di Gamberi, Cavolfiore, e Fagiolini

SHRIMP, CAULIFLOWER, AND GREEN BEAN SALAD · 140 CALORIES · 8.6 GR. CARBOHYDRATES

Spumoni di Pesche

PEACH SPUMONI · 125 CALORIES · 22.5 GR. CARBOHYDRATES

Total Calories
265

Total Carbohydrates
31.1 gr.

Insalata di Gamberi, Cavolfiore, e Fagiolini

SHRIMP, CAULIFLOWER, AND GREEN BEAN SALAD · 140 CALORIES · 8.6 GR. CARBOHYDRATES

INGREDIENTS

½ lb. cooked shrimp
1 small head of cauliflower
½ lb. fresh green beans

Tomato Vinaigrette Sauce:
1 tsp Dijon mustard
1 tsp red wine vinegar
1½ Tb olive oil
5 Tb diced fresh tomato (small dice)
1 tsp minced parsley

(Sauce continued)
1 tsp minced red onion
½ tsp minced fresh basil
½ tsp minced fresh mint
Salt and freshly ground pepper

Garnish:
4 large lettuce leaves
1 sliced hard-boiled egg
1 tsp minced parsley

METHOD

1. Divide cauliflower into 2 cups of bite-size flowerets, wash under cold running water.

2. Wash and string beans, then cut on a slight angle into 1½-inch lengths.

3. Boil cauliflower flowerets and green beans in separate pots of lightly salted water until tender but firm, approximately 2 minutes.

4. Pour the vegetables into a collander and run cold water over them to preserve fresh color. Drain well.

5. Combine shrimp and vegetables.

6. Place mustard and vinegar in a small mixing bowl. Beat with a whisk or a fork, adding oil gradually until oil is completely mixed in.

7. Add tomato, onion, basil, mint, and salt and pepper to taste.

8. Spoon vinaigrette sauce over salad. Stir carefully and allow to marinate in refrigerator for at least ½ hour.

9. Arrange salad attractively on beds of lettuce. Garnish with egg slices and a sprinkling of parsley.

Spumoni di Pesche

PEACH SPUMONI · 125 CALORIES · 22.5 GR. CARBOHYDRATES

INGREDIENTS

5 ripe, flavorful, fresh, medium-size peaches
2 tsp Marsala
1 tsp honey
1 envelope diet whipped-topping mix
½ cup cold non-fat milk
½ tsp vanilla

Garnish:
Fresh mint

METHOD

1. Plunge peaches into boiling water for 1 minute. Remove with a slotted spoon and peel.

2. Purée 3 peaches, add honey and Marsala.

3. Chop one peach into small dice and reserve the remaining peach for garnish.

4. Whip topping mix with milk and vanilla. You should have 1 cup of whipped topping.

5. Carefully fold purée and diced peaches into the whipped topping. Spoon mixture into stemmed sherbet glasses and place in freezer for 1 hour or until chilled and slightly firm.

6. Garnish with wedges of fresh peach and mint.

DINNER

Zuppa di Zucchine

ZUCCHINI SOUP · 62 CALORIES · 6.8 GR. CARBOHYDRATES

Petti di Tacchino Lisetta

TURKEY BREAST WITH BASIL AND TOMATOES · 194 CALORIES · 4.8 GR. CARBOHYDRATES

Crema Portoghese all'Amaretto

AMARETTO CUSTARD · 145 CALORIES · 21.2 GR. CARBOHYDRATES

Total Calories 401

Total Carbohydrates 32.8 gr.

Zuppa di Zucchine

ZUCCHINI SOUP · 62 CALORIES · 6.8 GR. CARBOHYDRATES

INGREDIENTS

1 lb. zucchini
¾ cup chopped onion
3 Tb water
1¾ cup chicken broth
2 cups water
Salt and pepper to taste
1 egg
1 Tb fresh chopped basil or parsley or 1½ tsp of each
2 Tb grated Parmesan cheese

METHOD

1. Wash zucchini thoroughly, cut off ends, and cut into slices ¼ inch thick.

2. Place 1 Tb water in a non-stick skillet, add onion, and sauté until soft, approximately 3 minutes.

3. Add zucchini slices and 2 Tb water and continue to sauté onions until zucchini and onions are lightly browned.

4. Place zucchini and onion in a heavy saucepan with cover and add chicken broth and water. Cover and simmer for approximately 30 minutes.

5. Purée vegetables and broth and return to saucepan. Add salt and pepper to taste.

6. Beat egg, herbs, and 1 Tb cheese together and place in a large bowl or soup tureen.

7. When ready to serve, pour boiling soup in a stream into the egg mixture, stirring constantly with a wire whisk.

8. Serve soup immediately, sprinkled with remaining cheese, or allow to cool and serve chilled.

Petti di Tacchino Lisetta

TURKEY BREAST WITH BASIL AND TOMATOES · 194 CALORIES · 4.8 GR. CARBOHYDRATES

INGREDIENTS

1 lb. turkey breast filets (boneless chicken breasts may be used)
4 ripe firm tomatoes
2 tsp olive oil
2 tsp minced garlic
6 or 8 fresh basil leaves (or 2 Tb minced parsley and ¼ tsp dry basil)
1 oz. shredded part-skim Mozzarella cheese
Salt and pepper to taste

METHOD

1. Sprinkle turkey filets lightly with salt and pepper and pound between pieces of waxed paper.

2. Plunge tomatoes into boiling water for 30 seconds to make peeling easier. Then peel and dice.

3. Sauté filets and garlic lightly in olive oil, using a non-stick skillet.

4. Stir in tomatoes and whole basil leaves and cook, stirring occasionally over medium heat until filets are just done and tomatoes slightly softened. Taste and add salt or pepper if needed.

5. Sprinkle with Mozzarella and toss until cheese is just melted.

6. This is a colorful dish and requires no other garnish. Serve at once.

Crema Portoghese all'Amaretto

AMARETTO CUSTARD · 145 CALORIES · 21.2 GR. CARBOHYDRATES

INGREDIENTS

3 Tb Amaretto liqueur
1¼ cup non-fat skim milk, or 4 Tb non-fat dry
2 eggs
4 tsp honey

1 Tb Amaretto liqueur
⅛ tsp vanilla
2 to 3 cups water

METHOD

1. Preheat oven to 350°.

2. Place 3 Tb Amaretto in a small heavy-bottomed saucepan. Bring to boil over medium heat and boil down until syrupy and caramel colored. Then pour into the bottom of 4 small custard cups or soufflé dishes and allow to cool.

3. Bring milk to a simmer in a small saucepan.

4. In a medium mixing bowl whisk eggs, honey, 1 Tb Amaretto, ⅛ tsp vanilla with a wire whisk until well blended.

5. Pour simmering milk into the eggs in a stream, whisking constantly, then pour liquid through a strainer into the custard cups.

6. Skim off any foam on top of the custard. Cover cups with aluminum foil and place the cups in a baking dish with sides at least as high as those of the custard cups.

7. Bring enough water to a boil in a kettle or saucepan to go ⅔ of the way up the sides of the cups.

8. Turn down oven to 325°.

9. Pour boiling water around the custard cups and place the baking dish in the lower ⅓ of the oven for 25 minutes or until custards are just set.

Note: Never let the water in the baking dish quite come to a simmer or custard will become grainy.

10. Remove custards from oven and set in a pan of cold water to cool. Refrigerate uncovered.

11. When ready to serve, unmold custards by running a sharp knife around the edges and placing cups in a pan of warm water for a few minutes before inverting the cups on dessert plates.

Potenza

BASILICATA

Cosenza

CALABRIA

Reggio di Calabria

CALABRIA and BASILICATA

LUNCHEON

Insalata di Arance e Cipolle

ORANGE AND ONION SALAD · 92 CALORIES · 15.7 GR. CARBOHYDRATES

Fusilli alla Pastora

SHEPHERD'S NOODLES · 175 CALORIES · 13.5 GR. CARBOHYDRATES

Formaggio Provolone e Uva

PROVOLONE CHEESE AND GRAPES · 157 CALORIES · 15.6 GR. CARBOHYDRATES

Total
Calories
424

Total
Carbohydrates
44.8 gr.

Insalata di Arance e Cipolle

ORANGE AND ONION SALAD · 92 CALORIES · 15.7 GR. CARBOHYDRATES

INGREDIENTS

3 oranges
8 thin slices of red onion divided into rings
1 Tb olive oil
Salt and freshly ground black pepper
4 leaves of lettuce (Bibb or Boston)

METHOD

1. Using a sharp knife, carefully peel oranges, removing white inner skin. Divide orange into skinless sections.

2. Place orange sections and onion rings in a bowl.

3. Sprinkle with olive oil and salt and black pepper to taste.

4. Allow salad to marinate for at least ½ hour before serving.

5. Place a lettuce leaf on each salad plate and arrange orange sections in a fan shape on lettuce. Top oranges with onions and spoon over any juice.

Fusilli alla Pastora

SHEPHERD'S NOODLES · 175 CALORIES · 31.5 GR. CARBOHYDRATES

INGREDIENTS

4 oz. uncooked Fusilli (noodles that resemble pulled-out watch springs) or other noodles
2 qt. water and 2 tsp salt
½ cup low-fat ricotta

Salt and freshly ground pepper
2 Tb grated Parmesan or Romano cheese
1 Tb coarsely chopped fresh basil or parsley

METHOD

1. Bring salted water to a rolling boil, add noodles, and cook until just tender, approximately 10 minutes.

2. While noodles are cooking, whip ricotta until smooth.

3. Mix ricotta with 3 or 4 Tb of the cooking water from the noodles, just enough to make a thick sauce. Season with salt and pepper to taste.

4. Drain noodles and toss with ricotta sauce.

5. Sprinkle with grated Parmesan or Romano, basil or parsley, and more pepper if desired. Serve immediately.

Formaggio Provolone e Uva

PROVOLONE CHEESE AND GRAPES · 157 CALORIES · 15.6 GR. CARBOHYDRATES

INGREDIENTS

1 oz. sharp Provolone per serving
½ cup grapes (Muscat or Thompson seedless) per serving

Provolone is a cheese now made in several regions of Italy, but traditionally typical of the southern regions. Made from either buffalo or cow's milk, it comes in two varieties—mild and sharp—and is sometimes also smoked.

The Provolone of Calabria, like many of the dishes typical of this region, is of the more piquant variety.

METHOD

1. On each plate, arrange thin slices of Provolone around a bunch of grapes.

DINNER

Zuppa di Cipolle

ONION SOUP · 104 CALORIES · 8.8 GR. CARBOHYDRATES

Gambe di Pollo Ripiene alla Lucana

STUFFED CHICKEN LEGS LUCANIAN STYLE · 226 CALORIES · 0.7 GR. CARBOHYDRATES

Tortoni Alessandra

BRANDIED CHOCOLATE TORTONI · 122 CALORIES · 13.8 GR. CARBOHYDRATES

Total Calories
452

Total Carbohydrates
23.3 gr.

Zuppa di Cipolle

ONION SOUP · 104 CALORIES · 8.8 GR. CARBOHYDRATES

INGREDIENTS

2 tsp butter
2 cups thinly sliced Bermuda onions
⅛ tsp sugar
Salt and pepper to taste
2 13¾-oz. cans beef broth
2 Tb brandy
2 slices diet bread
1½ Tb grated Romano cheese

METHOD

1. Melt butter in a non-stick skillet. Add onions, sugar and a light sprinkling of salt and pepper. Cook, stirring occasionally until onions are softened and translucent.

2. While onions are cooking, bring beef broth to a boil in a heavy saucepan.

3. Gradually stir 1 cup of boiling broth into the onions to deglaze, then return onions and broth to the saucepan.

4. Cover and simmer soup for 20 minutes.

5. Cut 4 rounds out of diet bread with a biscuit cutter, sprinkle with grated Romano, and place under a preheated broiler for a few seconds to brown. Reserve.

6. After 20 minutes, add 2 Tb of brandy to soup and continue to simmer for 5 minutes more.

7. Serve soup very hot with a toast round floating in each bowl. Sprinkle with remaining cheese.

Gambe di Pollo Ripiene alla Lucana

STUFFED CHICKEN LEGS LUCANIAN STYLE · 226 CALORIES · 0.7 GR. CARBOHYDRATES

INGREDIENTS

8 small chicken legs
4 oz. boneless breast of chicken
4 chicken livers
2 Tb grated Romano cheese
1 egg
¼ tsp salt
⅛ tsp pepper
Pinch rosemary
Pinch sage
1½ tsp olive oil
⅓ cup beef broth or water

Garnish:
1 large zucchini cut into match stick-like strips approximately 1 inch long
1 small red bell pepper cut into similar strips approximately 1 inch long
1½ tsp wine vinegar
1 Tb olive oil
1 Tb minced parsley
Salt and pepper

METHOD

1. Have the butcher bone the chicken legs or do it yourself.
a. Using a sharp knife, start at the large end of the drumstick and cut meat away from the knuckle.
b. Stand the drumstick on end and continue cutting downward, using a scraping motion with the blade of the knife toward the bone until the meat and skin are free of the bone.
c. Pull the bone toward you and out, turning the skin and meat inside out like a sweater sleeve.
d. With your knife, remove as many of the white sinew tendons as possible.
e. Turn the legs right side out again and tie the bottoms tightly with string. They are now ready for stuffing.

2. Chop chicken breast and liver into small pieces by hand or with a food processor. Stir in cheese, lightly beaten egg, salt, pepper, rosemary, and sage.

3. Divide mixture into eight parts and stuff legs. Secure the top of each one with string like a sausage link or fold over skin and secure with poultry lacers.

4. Preheat oven to 350°.

5. Brush a non-stick skillet with 1 tsp olive oil and brown chicken legs on all sides.

6. Place legs in a lightly oiled flameproof baking dish. Sprinkle with a little more salt, pepper, grated cheese, sage, and rosemary.

7. Bake in the center of preheated 350° oven for 30 minutes.

8. While chicken is cooking, toss zucchini and pepper strips with vinegar and oil, parsley, salt and pepper to taste, and a small pinch of sugar.

9. Remove chicken from baking dish and keep warm. Add water or broth to baking dish and place over low heat, scraping the bottom of dish to incorporate the cooking juices from chicken.

10. Place two drumsticks on each plate, spoon a little of the pan juices over them, and sprinkle with parsley. Garnish plates with vegetable strips and serve immediately.

Tortoni Alessandra

BRANDIED CHOCOLATE TORTONI · 122 CALORIES · 13.8 GR. CARBOHYDRATES

INGREDIENTS

½ cup skim milk
1 envelope low-calorie whipped topping
2 tsp chocolate extract
⅛ tsp vanilla extract
1 Tb brandy (optional)
2 egg whites
Pinch of salt

Optional garnish:
"chocolate leaves"
8 fresh mint or other nonpoisonous leaves
2 squares semi-sweet chocolate
4 drops of cooking oil
A pastry brush
Aluminum foil

Another possible garnish:
1 square of semi-sweet chocolate, grated

METHOD

1. Combine skim milk, whipped topping mix, chocolate extract, vanilla extract, and brandy in a medium-size mixing bowl. Beat until stiff.

2. In another bowl, beat egg whites.

3. Carefully fold egg whites into chocolate-cream mixture.

4. Spoon tortoni into 4 stemmed wine glasses or sherbet dishes and chill in the freezer for at least ½ hour.

5. To garnish, place chocolate squares in the top of a double boiler. Melt over boiling water and, when melted, stir in oil.

6. Wash and carefully dry leaves, then place face down on aluminum foil.

7. Dip pastry brush in chocolate and apply an even coat to back of leaves.

8. Carefully move coated leaves to a clean piece of foil if chocolate has extended over sides of leaf onto foil.

9. Chill leaves in the dryest part of your refrigerator until chocolate has hardened.

10. When ready to garnish, gently peel the real leaf off the chocolate leaf and place chocolate leaf carefully on tortoni.

Foggia

ADRIATIC SEA

Bari

BASILICATA

Brindisi

N

APULIA

LUNCHEON

Gamberi al Vino Bianco

SHRIMP IN WHITE WINE · 134 CALORIES · 3.0 GR. CARBOHYDRATES

Macedonia di Frutta

CHILLED FRUIT SALAD · 99 CALORIES · 29.1 GR. CARBOHYDRATES

Total
Calories
233

Total
Carbohydrates
32.1 gr.

Gamberi al Vino Bianco

SHRIMP IN WHITE WINE · 134 CALORIES · 3.0 GR. CARBOHYDRATES

INGREDIENTS

1 lb. raw shrimp, shelled and de-veined
2 tsp olive oil
2 tsp minced garlic
⅓ cup white wine
6 to 8 fresh whole basil leaves
1 oz. grated low-fat Mozzarella
Salt and pepper

Garnish:
4 lemon wedges

METHOD

1. Heat olive oil in a large non-stick skillet. Add garlic and shrimp and sauté over medium heat or until shrimp start to become opaque.

2. Add wine to skillet and continue cooking, stirring occasionally, for 1 minute or until wine has reduced by one half.

3. Sprinkle basil, Mozzarella, a few grindings of pepper and salt to taste over shrimp and toss together over low heat until cheese is melted.

4. Serve shrimp immediately on heated plates. Garnish with lemon wedges.

Macedonia di Frutta

CHILLED FRUIT SALAD · (WITHOUT LIQUEUR) 99 CALORIES · 29.1 GR. CARBOHYDRATES

INGREDIENTS

1 orange
1 pear
1 unblemished red eating apple
1 banana
½ cup orange juice
1½ Tb lemon juice
1 tsp grated lemon rind
1 Tb maraschino liqueur (optional: 11 calories · 1.1 grams carbohydrates more per serving)

METHOD

1. Using a sharp knife, carefully peel orange, making sure to remove white inner skin. Cut orange into sections.

2. Peel pear and cut into bite-size pieces.

3. Cut unpeeled apple into bite-size pieces.

4. Peel and cut banana into rounds.

5. Combine fruit with orange juice, lemon juice, lemon rind, and optional liqueur.

6. Serve chilled fruit macedonia in compotes or wine glasses.

DINNER

Rigatoni al Cavolfiore

RIGATONI NOODLES WITH CAULIFLOWER · 168 CALORIES · 26.1 GR. CARBOHYDRATES

Sogliole al Piatto

STEAMED SOLE APULIA STYLE · 185 CALORIES · 1.5 GR. CARBOHYDRATES

Sorbetto di Arance e Limoni

ORANGE AND LEMON SHERBET · 89 CALORIES · 26.0 GR. CARBOHYDRATES

Total
Calories
442

Total
Carbohydrates
53.6 gr.

Rigatoni al Cavolfiore

RIGATONI NOODLES WITH CAULIFLOWER · 168 CALORIES · 26.1 GR. CARBOHYDRATES

INGREDIENTS

2 qts. water and 2 tsp salt
1⅓ cup dry Mezzani Rigatoni 4 noodles or other similar pasta
2 cups cauliflower flowerets (wash cauliflower and divide into flowerets)
1 tsp minced garlic
1 tsp olive oil

1½ cups whole canned Italian-style tomatoes and juice
¼ tsp dry Italian Seasonings
1 Tb minced parsley
2 Tb grated Parmesan cheese
Salt and pepper

METHOD

1. Bring salted water to a rolling boil in the bottom of a large spaghetti cooker with steaming basket (if you don't have a steamer, use two saucepans, each with 2 quarts of water and 2 tsp salt).

2. Put noodles into the boiling water and place the cauliflower flowerets in the steamer basket above (cauliflower can also be boiled separately). Noodles should be cooked for 12 to 15 minutes.

3. Steam or boil cauliflower flowerets for approximately 5 minutes or until just tender. Remove half of the cauliflower and reserve for garnish. Continue cooking remaining cauliflower for 2 minutes more.

4. While noodles and cauliflower are cooking, sauté garlic in olive oil, using a non-stick skillet. Do not color. Stir in tomatoes, juice, and Italian Seasonings. Cook over medium heat, stirring often for 7 minutes.

5. Remove second half of flowerets from steamer and add to tomatoes. Cook together for 1 minute, then purée to make a sauce. If the sauce is too thick, add enough cooking water from the noodles to reach the desired consistency. Season with salt and pepper to taste.

6. Drain noodles and combine with the sauce and half of grated cheese and parsley.

7. Sprinkle with remaining cheese and serve immediately.

Sogliole al Piatto

STEAMED SOLE APULIA STYLE · 185 CALORIES · 1.5 GR. CARBOHYDRATES

INGREDIENTS

4 6-oz. sole filets
2 tsp minced garlic
4 tsp minced parsley
4 tsp olive oil
Salt and pepper

Garnish:
2 tsp minced parsley
4 lemon wedges
4 small bouquets of watercress

METHOD

1. Wash filets under cold running water. Pat dry with paper towels.

2. Combine garlic, parsley, and oil in a small bowl.

3. Bring water to a boil in the bottom of a steamer.

4. Spread ½ of garlic mixture on one side of filets and sprinkle lightly with salt and pepper.

5. Place filets, seasoned side down, in the steamer basket and spread remaining mixture on the other side. Sprinkle with salt and pepper.

6. Cover and steam fish for one or two minutes, just until the filets are firm and opaque.

7. Sprinkle lightly with minced parsley and garnish plates with lemon wedges and watercress bouquets.

Sorbetto di Arance e Limoni

ORANGE AND LEMON SHERBET · 89 CALORIES · 26.0 GR. CARBOHYDRATES · SERVES 6

INGREDIENTS

4 oranges = 1¼ cup juice
2 lemons = ½ cup juice
1 Tb orange zest (peel), cut into thin strips, and 1 Tb lemon zest
    cut into thin strips
1¾ cups water
3 Tb honey

Garnish:
4 thin orange slices
4 fresh mint leaves

METHOD

1. Strain the orange and lemon juices.

2. Combine the orange and lemon zest with water and honey in a heavy-bottomed saucepan. Bring to a simmer, stirring often with a wire whisk, then allow to cool.

3. Pour honied water through a strainer into fruit juice, thus removing zest.

4. Chill the mixture for at least 1 hour, then put into the ice-cream maker and follow the directions for your type of machine.

Note: If using the ice-tray freezing method, see recipe for Pear Ice (page 30).

5. If you are using the type of electric ice-cream maker that fits in your freezer, remove the sherbet from the freezer one hour before serving and allow to soften somewhat in the refrigerator.

6. Spoon into champagne or wine glasses and garnish with mint leaves.

Palermo
Marsala
Taormina
Agrigento
Syracuse

N

SICILY

LUNCHEON

Tortino di Melanzane

EGGPLANT PIE · 192 CALORIES · 8.6 GR. CARBOHYDRATES

Arance Dolci

ORANGES WITH CINNAMON · 78 CALORIES · 20.0 GR. CARBOHYDRATES

Total Calories 270

Total Carbohydrates 28.6 gr.

Tortino di Melanzane

EGGPLANT PIE · 192 CALORIES · 8.6 GR. CARBOHYDRATES

INGREDIENTS

2 qt. boiling water
1 medium eggplant, approximately ½ lb.
1 tsp minced garlic
2 tsp olive oil
Salt and pepper to taste
1 tsp olive oil
3 Tb minced onion
2 cups peeled chopped tomatoes
1 Tb minced parsley

¼ tsp dry Italian Seasonings
1 tsp capers
Salt and pepper to taste
4 oz thinly sliced low-fat Mozzarella
3 tomato slices
2 eggs
2 egg whites
1 pinch salt
1 Tb grated Romano cheese

METHOD

1. Preheat oven to 375°.

2. Wash eggplant and slice into rounds ½ inch thick. Parboil slices for 3 minutes, then pat dry, squeezing out moisture with paper towels.

3. Heat 2 tsp oil in non-stick skillet and add minced garlic and a layer of eggplant slices. Brown slices on both sides and sprinkle lightly with salt and pepper.

4. Cover the bottom of a 10-inch lightly oiled or non-stick pie plate with eggplant slices, allowing the slices to go partly up the sides of the dish.

5. Place pie plate in the oven while you prepare the tomato mixture.

6. Heat 1 tsp olive oil in non-stick skillet, add onion, and sauté until lightly softened, but not colored.

7. Add chopped tomato, parsley, Italian Seasonings, and salt and pepper. Cook over medium heat, stirring often until sauce cooks down and thickens slightly, about 10 minutes.

8. Remove eggplant from the oven and cover eggplant slices with a thin layer of Mozzarella, then top with tomato slices.

9. Place whole eggs in a medium-size mixing bowl. Whisk until light and frothy.

10. Beat egg whites and salt together in a separate bowl until they stand in soft peaks.

11. Stir tomato mixture into whole eggs. Add capers and salt and pepper if necessary.

12. Carefully fold whites into tomato-egg mixture until thoroughly incorporated.

13. Pour egg-tomato mixture into pie plate and bake in the middle of preheated oven for 20 minutes.

14. Sprinkle with grated Parmesan and return to oven for 5 or 10 minutes more or until eggs are thoroughly set and top lightly browned.

15. Cut pie into wedges and serve at once.

Arance Dolci

ORANGES WITH CINNAMON · 78 CALORIES · 20.0 GR. CARBOHYDRATES

INGREDIENTS

4 oranges
1 tsp lemon juice
Cinnamon to taste

METHOD

1. Peel oranges, removing all white inner skin.

2. Holding a peeled orange over a bowl to catch juice, cut between section membranes with a small sharp knife and let sections fall into bowl.

3. Squeeze the remaining membranes to remove any juice. Discard membranes. Continue in the same manner with remaining oranges.

4. Add 1 tsp lemon juice to orange sections and sprinkle with cinnamon to taste.

5. Check for sweetness and add honey (61 calories · 16.5 gr carbohydrates per Tb) to taste if necessary.

DINNER

Spaghetti all'Agrodolce

SPAGHETTI WITH SWEET AND SOUR SAUCE · 163 CALORIES · 19.5 GR. CARBOHYDRATES

Bracciola alla Siciliana

ROLLED STUFFED FLANK STEAK · 257 CALORIES · 9.6 GR. CARBOHYDRATES

Sorbetto di Banana

BANANA SHERBET · 63 CALORIES · 17.1 GR. CARBOHYDRATES

Total Calories 483

Total Carbohydrates 46.2 gr.

Spaghetti all'Agrodolce

SPAGHETTI WITH SWEET AND SOUR SAUCE
163 CALORIES · 19.5 GR. CARBOHYDRATES

INGREDIENTS

4 oz. dry spaghetti
1 Tb salt
2 qt. water
1 tsp olive oil

METHOD

1. Bring water to a rapid boil, add salt, oil, and spaghetti. Cook until tender, but not soft. Drain.

2. Serve as a first course with Sauce Agrodolce. See recipe Bracciola Siciliana (page 130).

Bracciola alla Siciliana

ROLLED STUFFED FLANK STEAK · 257 CALORIES · 9.6 GR. CARBOHYDRATES

INGREDIENTS

1 16-oz. flank steak trimmed of all fat
1 lb. fresh spinach or 1 10-oz. package frozen
    spinach
1 tsp minced garlic
1 oz. raisins
Salt, pepper, and nutmeg to taste
2 hard-boiled eggs
1 tsp olive oil

Sauce Agrodolce:
1 tsp olive oil
¾ cup chopped onion

2 tsp chopped parsley
2 tsp chopped fresh basil or ½ tsp dry
2 cups canned tomatoes
1 cup juice from can
1½ tsp honey dissolved in 2 tsp wine vinegar
¼ tsp cinnamon
½ tsp salt or to taste
¼ tsp pepper or to taste

Garnish:
Watercress bouquet and fresh mushroom slices

METHOD

1. Sprinkle flank steak lightly with salt and pepper.

2. Remove large stems from fresh spinach and wash. Place in a covered saucepan with just the water clinging to the leaves and cook until barely wilted, approximately 1 minute.

3. Squeeze spinach to remove as much water as possible, then purée along with 1 tsp minced garlic. Season with salt, pepper, and nutmeg.

4. Place the steak on a cutting board or cookie sheet with one of the narrow ends toward you.

5. Spread a layer of spinach on the steak, leaving a border 1-inch wide around the edges free of spinach.

6. Sprinkle a layer of raisins on top of spinach, then place whole hard-boiled eggs end to end across the end of steak nearest to you.

7. Roll the steak up with the eggs inside, folding in the side edges to keep stuffing from escaping. Tie the roll with string or use toothpicks to make a neat bundle.

8. Brown steak roll in a non-stick skillet with 1 tsp olive oil, then remove to a Dutch oven or large heavy saucepan with lid.

9. Place 1 tsp of oil in the skillet and add chopped onion, parsley, and basil. Cook, stirring occasionally, until onion is golden.

10. Then stir in tomatoes, juice, cinnamon, salt, pepper, and honey dissolved in vinegar.

11. Pour sauce over steak, bring to a boil, then cover. Turn heat down to a simmer for 1½ hours, or until steak is tender.

12. Remove steak and keep warm.

13. Let sauce boil down uncovered until thick. Serve with ½ cup cooked spaghetti per person as a first course.

14. Remove string or toothpicks and cut steak into 8 slices. Serve on plates garnished with watercress and mushroom slices.

Sorbetto di Banana

BANANA SHERBET · 63 CALORIES · 17.1 GR. CARBOHYDRATES · SERVES 6

INGREDIENTS

1 cup mashed banana (approximately 2 medium bananas)
3 Tb honey
Juice of 1 lemon
1 cup cold water

Garnish:
Mint leaves

METHOD

1. Place banana, honey, and lemon juice in a blender or food processor. Blend until smooth.

2. Gradually add water while blending until mixture is light and fluffy.

3. Freeze mixture in an ice-cream freezer following the instructions for your machine, or pour into ice trays that have been thoroughly washed with boiling water and rinsed with cold water and baking soda to remove all odors.

4. If using the ice-tray method, fill trays only ⅔ full and stir the sherbet with a whisk or fork 2 or 3 times during the freezing process to make it fluffier in texture.

5. Spoon sherbet into stemmed wine glasses and garnish with fresh mint.

·A·N·T·I·P·A·S·T·I·

VERDURE MISTE

ANTIPASTI

Verdure Miste

BOUQUET OF RAW VEGETABLES · 4 CALORIES · 2.6 GR. CARBOHYDRATES

Salsa di Salmone

SMOKED SALMON DIP · 20 CALORIES · 0.1 GR. CARBOHYDRATES

Uove Sode Ripiene

STUFFED EGGS · 33 CALORIES · 0.3 GR. CARBOHYDRATES

Frittatine

INDIVIDUAL ZUCCHINI OMELETTES · 20 CALORIES · 0.6 GR. CARBOHYDRATES

Caponata

COLD EGGPLANT RELISH · 45 CALORIES · 5.8 GR. CARBOHYDRATES

Gnocchi Verdi

SPINACH DUMPLINGS · 11 CALORIES · 0.6 GR. CARBOHYDRATES

Carote Margherita

MARINATED CARROTS · 23 CALORIES · 1.2 GR. CARBOHYDRATES

Verdure Miste

BOUQUET OF RAW VEGETABLES
APPROXIMATELY 4 CALORIES · 2.6 GR. CARBOHYDRATES PER VEGETABLE FLOWER

INGREDIENTS

1 head red cabbage
2 bunches large scallions (green onions)
2 bunches radishes
3 or 4 very small purple and white turnips
1 head cauliflower
1 head broccoli
1 zucchini
1 cucumber
2 small yellow squash
1 box cherry tomatoes

1 large red bell pepper
6 large pitted black olives

Equipment:
1 vase (large enough to hold a red cabbage)
3 doz. bamboo barbecue skewers of different lengths, dyed green with food color, boiling water, and vinegar
1 small sharp paring knife
1 radish rose cutter (optional)

METHOD

Note: Scallions, radishes, and turnips should be carved at least 2 hours in advance and placed in ice water to open. They can be made 2 or 3 days in advance and stored in cold water in the refrigerator. See carving instructions.

1. Wash all vegetables thoroughly in cold water.

2. Place red cabbage in vase and bend back leaves like petals.

3. Starting at the top center, stick the dull end of bamboo skewers into the cabbage in a uniform pattern, covering its entire surface (as if arranging flowers).

4. Cut off single scallion leaves to slip over and cover the skewers, leaving the point exposed. This makes the stems of flowers.

Vegetable Carving Instructions:
   Scallions (green onions):

1. Cut off the bulb end about 3 inches down into the green.

2. Slice off root.

3. Form petals by cutting around the bulb to a depth of ¾ of an inch, continuing in decreasing circles until you reach the center (see diagram).

4. Place in cold water to open, then place on skewers.

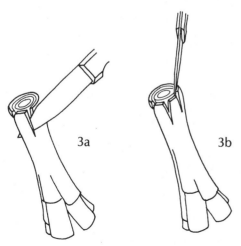
3a   3b

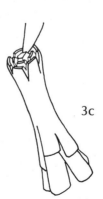
3c

4

Radishes:

1. Cut off root tips, stems, and leaves.

2. Wash in cold water.

3. Use a radish rose cutter or make the flowers described below:

a. Radish Mum: Use the roundest radishes for this flower. Hold the radish stem-side down. Make a series of cuts ¾ of the depth of the radish all across the top. Turn the radish clockwise and carefully make similar cuts crisscross to the first ones.

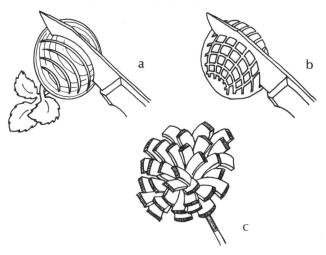

b. Radish Tulip: Use long radishes for this flower. Hold the radish stem-side down. Starting at the tip of the radish with the point of your knife, cut a thin petal-shaped slice. Then, turning radish, cut 3 or 4 more petals. If you wish to make a more elaborate flower, continue to cut more petals in the white part of the radish in decreasing circles.

4. Drop in cold water to open, then place on skewers.

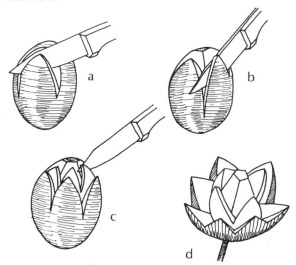

Turnip Blossom:

1. Holding turnip stem-end down, make v-shaped cuts ¼ inch deep all around the lower ⅓ of the unpeeled turnip, making a zigzag pattern.

2. Place the point of your knife under the top point of each zigzag and carefully open the "petal."

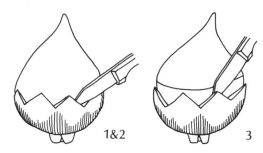

1&2   3

3. Carefully round off the turnip, removing all peel except that in the opened petals, and cut out a space behind the petals.

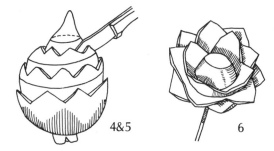

4&5   6

4. Make cuts like those described in Step 1, into the white part of the turnip and round the turnip again, making a space behind the new row of petals.

5. Continue in this fashion until you reach the top of the turnip.

6. Drop in cold water to open, then place on skewers.

Broccoli and Cauliflower Blossoms:

1. Divide into bite-size flowerets. The natural shape resembles a flower.

2. Place on skewers.

135

Zucchini and Cucumber Lollipops:

1. Score the sides of an unpeeled zucchini or cucumber with a fork and cut into rounds ¼ inch thick.

2. Cut a ¼-inch wide notch to the center in the outside edge of each round.

3. Holding rounds at right angles to each other, fit notches together and place on a skewer.

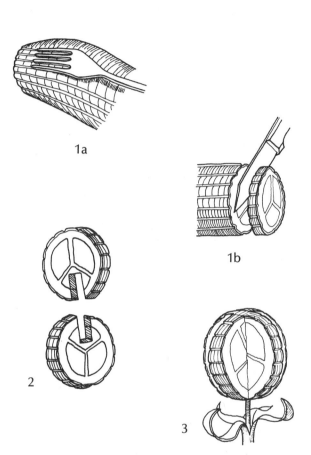

1a

1b

2

3

Yellow Crooked Neck Squash Blossoms:

1. Cut unpeeled squash in half—one flower can be made from each end, using the end as the flower's base.

2. Using the technique described for the Turnip Blossoms, steps 1 through 3, cut v-shaped petals, open them, and round off the white inside flesh above and behind them.

3. Carefully make one more row of petals in the soft white flesh.

4. Place flowers on skewers.

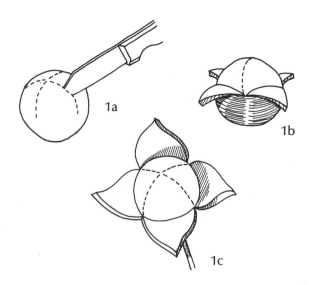

1a

1b

1c

Cherry Tomato Tulips:

Must be prepared at the last minute.

1. Cut a cross on the top of each tomato and carefully peel back skin, forming 4 petals.

2. Place on skewers.

Olive and Bell Pepper Blossoms:

1. Cut pepper into strips 1½ inches long and 1 inch wide.

2. Make fringe-like cuts 1 inch deep into the length of each strip.

3. Roll strip and place, fringe end out, in the center of each olive.

4. Place olives on skewers.

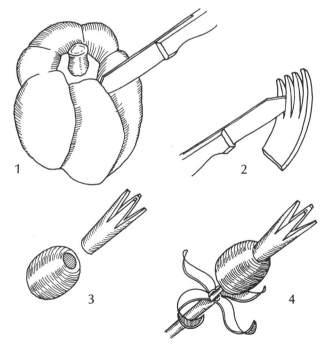

1

2

3

4

Salsa di Salmone

SMOKED SALMON DIP
APPROXIMATELY 20 CALORIES · 0.1 GR. CARBOHYDRATES PER SERVING
APPROXIMATELY 50 SERVINGS OF DIP

INGREDIENTS

1 16-oz. can red salmon, drained, skin and bones removed
¼ lb. smoked salmon
3 Tb minced onion
2 tsp lemon juice
2 tsp horse-radish
1 Tb capers
1 anchovy filet (optional)
3 to 4 Tb low-fat yogurt
Salt and pepper to taste

METHOD

1. Purée salmon, onion, lemon juice, horse-radish, capers, and anchovy in a blender or food processor.

2. Put salmon mixture in a medium-size mixing bowl and fold in yogurt to thin dip to desired consistency.

3. Add salt and pepper to taste.

4. Serve chilled as a special low-calorie dip for raw vegetables.

Uove Sode Ripiene

STUFFED EGGS · 33 CALORIES · 0.3 GR. CARBOHYDRATES · MAKES 24 CANAPES

INGREDIENTS

1 doz. small eggs
4 Tb low-fat plain yogurt
½ tsp Dijon mustard
2 Tb minced onion
½ tsp anchovy paste (optional)
1 Tb chopped capers
2 tsp minced fresh basil

1 tsp minced parsley
Salt and pepper to taste

Garnish:
1 Tb whole capers
6 thin slices of unpeeled cucumber
24 tiny strips of pimento

METHOD

1. Put eggs in a saucepan of cold water. Bring to a boil and boil slowly for 8 minutes.

2. Plunge eggs into a bowl of cold water to cool and peel when cool.

3. Cut a very thin slice off each end of eggs so that they will stand. Cut eggs in half across the width and carefully remove the yolks without damaging the whites.

4. Set whites aside on serving platter.

5. Mash or purée yolks and combine with the remaining ingredients except garnish.

6. Using pastry bag with a star tip, or a spoon, fill the cavities of reserved egg whites.

7. Cut cucumber slices into fourths or sixths, depending on their size.

8. Garnish each bite-size deviled egg with 2 capers, a strip of pimento, and a tiny cucumber "fan."

9. Refrigerate if you are preparing the eggs in advance, but serve at room temperature.

Frittatine di Zucchine

INDIVIDUAL ZUCCHINI OMELETTES
20 CALORIES · 0.6 GR. CARBOHYDRATES · MAKES 16 SERVINGS

INGREDIENTS

½ lb. zucchini
¼ tsp salt
1 tsp butter
1½ Tb minced scallion (green onion)
2 tsp minced parsley

3 eggs
Pepper and cayenne to taste
1 Tb grated Parmesan or Romano cheese
Paprika
1 non-stick muffin tin

METHOD

1. Preheat oven to 400°.

2. Scrub zucchini thoroughly under cold running water, but do not peel.

3. Grate zucchini and toss with ¼ tsp salt.

4. Put into a collander to drain for ½ hour. Then squeeze out any remaining juice.

5. Melt 1 tsp butter in a non-stick skillet. Add zucchini and onion. Sauté lightly.

6. Beat parsley and eggs together in a small mixing bowl. Stir in zucchini and onion. Add pepper and cayenne to taste.

7. Spoon 1 Tb of omelette mixture into each section of the muffin tin. Divide any remaining mixture evenly.

8. Bake in the middle of preheated oven for 5 minutes or until omelettes begin to pull away from the sides of tin.

9. Run a small sharp knife around the edges of each omelette to loosen it.

10. Sprinkle lightly with grated cheese and paprika.

11. Put under the broiler for a few seconds until top is lightly browned.

12. Serve omelettes hot or at room temperature.

Caponata

COLD EGGPLANT RELISH · 45 CALORIES · 5.8 GR. CARBOHYDRATES · SERVES 10

INGREDIENTS

1 lb. eggplant
Salt
4 tsp olive oil
1 cup finely chopped celery
1 to 2 Tb water
½ cup red wine vinegar mixed with 1½ tsp honey
1½ cup drained canned Italian-style whole tomatoes

⅓ cup juice from tomatoes
1 Tb capers
¼ tsp anchovy paste
1 Tb raisins
Salt and freshly ground black pepper to taste

Garnish:
2 tsp freshly minced parsley

METHOD

1. Cut the ends off an unpeeled eggplant. Cut eggplant into 1-inch cubes.

2. Sprinkle the cubes with salt and place on a bed of paper towels. Put a plate or a cutting board on top of eggplant to help press out bitter juice. Allow to sit for 30 minutes.

3. Heat 2 tsp olive oil in a large non-stick skillet and add the celery. Cook over moderate heat, stirring often, for 5 minutes.

4. Add onion to the skillet and continue to cook for another 8 to 10 minutes, or until celery and onion are soft and lightly colored. If the mixture becomes very dry, add 1 to 2 Tb of water during cooking.

5. Remove celery and onion to a bowl with a slotted spoon.

6. Rinse eggplant cubes under cold running water. Pat dry with more paper towels.

7. Heat remaining 2 tsp oil in the skillet and add the eggplant. Sauté over medium heat, turning the cubes constantly for 8 to 10 minutes or until lightly browned on all sides.

8. Return the celery and onions to the skillet and stir in vinegar and honey, drained tomatoes, tomato juice, capers, anchovy paste, raisins, and a light sprinkling of salt and pepper.

9. Bring to a boil, reduce heat, and simmer uncovered, stirring frequently, for 15 minutes.

10. Taste the caponata and adjust seasonings, adding more salt, pepper, or vinegar if necessary.

11. Transfer to a serving bowl and refrigerate.

12. Serve caponata cold, sprinkled with fresh minced parsley.

Gnocchi Verdi

SPINACH DUMPLINGS · 11 CALORIES · 0.6 GR. CARBOHYDRATES · MAKES 32 SERVINGS

INGREDIENTS

1 recipe of Gnocchi Verdi, see page 60.
3 Tb grated Romano cheese
Paprika to taste

METHOD

1. Make gnocchi according to the instructions on page 60 and place in a buttered baking dish.

2. Preheat oven to 350°.

3. Sprinkle gnocchi with grated Romano cheese and paprika. Cover with foil and bake for 10 minutes, or until hot, in the middle of preheated 350° oven.

4. Serve with frilled toothpicks.

Carote Margherita

MARINATED CARROTS · 23 CALORIES · 1.2 GR. CARBOHYDRATES

INGREDIENTS

½ lb. baby carrots (approximately 15 carrots)
1 Tb finely sliced scallions (green onions both green and white parts)
1 Tb minced parsley (Italian broad leaf if possible)
⅛ tsp oregano or to taste
Salt and pepper to taste
2½ tsp red wine vinegar
2 Tb olive oil

Garnish:
Parsley

METHOD

1. Peel the carrots and cook in lightly salted boiling water for 8 to 10 minutes, or until easily pierced with a knife but still firm.

2. Drain the carrots and place in a serving dish.

3. Sprinkle onion, parsley, oregano, salt, and pepper over carrots.

4. Pour oil and vinegar over carrots. Toss lightly.

5. Allow carrots to marinate for at least 3 to 4 hours at room temperature before serving. If marinating for longer than 4 hours, refrigerate, but serve at room temperature.

6. Turn carrots in the marinade from time to time.

7. Serve carrots in the marinade and garnish with parsley.

Index